# THEY CAME FROM THE STARS

F.R. O'REGAN

*This book, I'm dedicating to the guides who believed in me to come, to Michael, my friend in the other world, and to Dean, Rhaji and to Lee-Anne who is brave enough to come out as a spiritual medium and say I believe in off-world guides and guardians when very few are. And Brighidin, the fun with Jim helping from the other world. This early morning waking has to stop.*

*I'm also dedicating this to my Animal work, to all who know they come from the stars. And to the colourful people of my world who stand and hold the space, who stand and say I'm not different because of who I love. This subject came in strong throughout all three books, I didn't understand at the beginning I do now. This dedication is for them.*

*Our world is made up of all the colours of the Rainbow, and yet so is the universe.*

# FOREWORD

*If you have read Alive and free a Leap of Faith you will know that we have a Medium from the spirit world assisting in the writing of these books, we call him MF. And a friend and regressionist in the lifetime called MN, and many friends that started off as guides. Dean is the one and Rhaji. You will meet them all in this book.*

*No names of Helpers from spirit have been used in these books; it was my only stipulation when I agreed to Channel them. Some have asked to keep their names, for the simple reason, in their own words it was a life, and I am just a soul.*

*Others have described their lives, with again other names to protect living loved ones.*

*In this book all are off world except a couple, one is MF and MN. E. However, he does not mind if you know who he is we just left the channels as they came in.*

*Many channels I struggled to believe myself, I have got used to them now, and fully believe these off-world guides and Guardians. As with Alive and Free series, I will say only this.*

*If It resonates keep the information stored in your mind, if not let it go.*

*As Dean would say, no one is forcing you Author.*

*Dean comes first in this book, as he was the guide I struggled to get on with the most. In truth, we were both as bad as each other.*

*All channels are laid out as I was told, no word changes only edit of punctuation and grammar, I felt I would have some leeway on this one till I started to edit and got told off. I hear Don't you dare just as soon as I try to bring them up to date.*

1

# FROM ONE MEDIUM TO ANOTHER

**MF:** Alright so it's not morning its lunchtime on your Earthside today. The snow is still annoying you I see.

**Author:** Not in the sense of annoying me, but my Daughters car parked up.

**MF:** Yes, she was extremely lucky yesterday as I have it your father her grandfather, is working overtime right now with you both driving in bad weather. You said you felt it was the hand of God that stopped your car going over that ditch, you wouldn't be far wrong but not "god" Our Archangels sending plenty to your Earthside right now.

Before we start let me give you some insight into the goings on right now. You have asked For Dr Mn to be here and he will be along shortly. I know his exuberance, and childlike energy around things he hasn't seen is contagious, and though his earthwork took him to many areas of our world; going off planet never occurred in many lives he worked with. But here and now he can experience this. So yes, we will be attended by him shortly.

Readings Author in all their work, for you and the

spirit person who comes, is proving life after death, proving the soul (points to chest) is still living in the here and now, not you're here and now ours. The soul is still learning. Also, I do not know all just because I died. I do not know, all just because I'm a higher consciousness soul compared to many. I am learning also. I can channel because as a soul I worked with my guides upon the Earth side of life and was trance there. The trance is proving the soul lives on. We applaud that.

Now when your Training Mediums become bored giving Readings, it's time to shake them up. I get that we are fed up, and you have gone through the exact same. Many are taking thirty years to get to that point, some like yourself not that long, it's the conscious mind as you move up in consciousness your less able to tolerate lower energy forces. And some of the souls you read are just that, lower energy younger souls.

While the evidence is good, it becomes boring. Move these on to other training Mediums, who can learn to reach that consciousness level your bored with and challenge yourself. Ask for higher souls to come into be read, guides Guardians and Archangels. Also, ask for souls who have passed in the life you are not connected to. Many of us will come we still have a voice. So, ask to speak to Nikola Tesla. Ask to speak to Dolores Cannon. Ask to speak to Sir Isaac Newton. Because they will come. They have so much experience they wish to help you all with.

They lived that lifetime, so requesting is all well and good, but the same soul has to want to return to that life to glean the knowledge to again pass it on. Ask to speak to the captain of the Titanic those who built her, and the list goes on, it's all viable to be able to do so. Now, this is where you hold the advantage you have done this, along with other mediums and channels. By sheer bloody-mindedness and when Johan said yes you could, you said well show me.

It will take Mediums with the nerve, but also the need to give these souls something back, not just a voice to give them back the Anonymity to allow them to work with you. But by allowing them to give you information about your work that only their loved ones would know them. This is letting them know you're working with them without gaining from it, and families Earthside do not want us taken advantage of and rightly so. I know you work solely on this aspect or not at all, I just would like others to see that it can be done. And when this book goes out, I know, we will be called into work. I will never give evidential Mediumship through a medium to connect to my family my soulmate, we have spoken about this, but as this information will go out. I'm correcting and saying again you do not mind me taking up your work time, do you?

**Author** *God No tear away. It's your platform.*

**MF:** There is a red boxer here in spirit she was ours along with a French bulldog, I do not give names many would do well to remember that. And remember when you laughed at me Author for having time to come work with me as I'm meant to be somewhere else. Well, I was never somewhere else. Do not get me wrong I have helped from this side but only touched on, not helped or certainly never channelled as we do. I do have no desire to be famous here for heaven's sake I worked enough there.

I am letting my Husband know it's alright to move on, and love someone else, but I am a soul mate, and when you come home, you know this. It's alright move on and be with others for companionship, and I encourage this, you are not expected to live the remainder of your life in solitude, yes animals are not living alone, but he knows as I know it's alright, we spoke about this.

Matching tattoos, I keep mine. And stepping out of the limelight, I know my "family" I use this term loosely as its guilt and bad karma they are clocking up. Move on my love and let it be.

Author lets work.

Author, we have a good day set up. For you today.

See that pink auric field around that moon ahead. We are going there.

**Author**. *My head is exploding with the higher energy, give me a minute to help it settle. I feel sick too. Couple minutes later have had to close the curtains and drink water head sore, But its levelling out now.*

**MF: Are** you alright now being you ready to go?

**Author**: *Gosh what's happened today your so impatient give me a minute, or we get no work done?*

**Higher Guide.** I stand before you in my true form Medium. You come to my planet. This is erm surprising; the energy didn't blow your head off. Metaphorically, of course, I did see you struggle slightly, and your Medium Guide here was pretentious bringing you here. Thinking you would cope, but now we know you can it will open the world up for us to help you understand it.

**Author**...*My head is cold around the top. How blooming strange the feeling, I feel.*

**MF:** I wasn't pretentious, I was hoping you could cope with the elevated levels in energy I suspected you could, And I'm sorry we have left Mn behind but will work with him later the energy levels to high right now. Relax, more water Author. Then we go on. Before this Guide has a blue fit.

**Higher Guide.** That is a strange name you call me, but I deserve it I have offered you no details, and as we are to be "friends" I will give you such details at a time when it suits me. (**Author:** *I called him an ET. Guide*) Human feelings and such tragedies of the human mind are alien to me. I do not feel them like others would it's Our non-free will world there is no time to decide how to feel around such simple things in our lives. We work with high energy octaves always that the lowly I suppose is not seen or explained to us as we grow. I feel I will irritate you with having no time for small-mindedness on your planet Medium; I know your name, and I have been told anonymity goes both ways. I know you wish to keep my details secret if it required, I think not I do not mind if others know who we are, as we have been hidden from your world for a long time, no long does not suit Aeons or a Millennia of time-based on the Earth world as our time is measured so much different.

On our world you wouldn't survive in the body you have been entrusted to for your, Earth world, so when you're born in the spiritual world you are given a body suitable for the Planets you will inhabit, I haven't lost you yet?

**Author.** *Nope, keep going I'm here.*

**Higher Guide.** Your Human body is based on the Parental bodies of choice; then this lives DNA of choice based on the parental, they give you three body choices sometimes more sometimes less, for the contract chosen. Less energy less per cent of soul energy needed. The body is sluggish the life demanding, and the body is done by the time comes for you to return.

The souls who choose to come to our world are all on the same Body chose and DNA the same; the only differed are personalities. I am stoic I know this, I travel to your Spiritual world to take the new souls' home to my world to teach them Energy work. These are your Mediums and Inventors and Doctors and Veterinary careers of the Earth world. Yes, some stand out, others do not, this is the same all over. We have a good working relationship with each other; we send some of ours also your spiritual world to learn humility, granted it's not needed.

But we learn it. As another reason to work, we also have incarnating souls on your world. These souls are the pioneers the Mediums and the Inventors we have many souls in various "jobs" on the Earth world, they have a total encompassing block on their memories, so they cannot know where they come from after all a soul is a soul right?

**Author:** *Why are you Channelling to our world, what do we need to know?*

**Higher Guide.** This is very simple, while many of your Mediums and psychics and lightworkers are meditating Daily and quieting their minds your Spiritual world and guides are opening their minds to the possibilities of the fluffy and soft side to Spirit. They are also choosing the messengers who will awake the world to the possibility of us, of life outside of your own. They are teaching channels and trance workers to channel us. We prefer telepathic communication but will work through channel also. Your mediums and Lightworkers are learning to connect to their higher self. They are learning to follow the direction of the guides who lived before them or with them. They are teaching humanity to all and hope that they will wake up and teach others.

**Author**: *Do you see a time when the world is awake?*

**Higher Guide.** (Laughs)Medium I dislike being the one to keep telling you to look at the divide. The great divide what is human in the making. The divide where on the soul is on onside and one on the other. Driven by greed Hate, intolerance. Need want, and many other Human needs want and desire.

To be human is to love and understand to tolerate, and to show the way into the light. To be human is humanity and humans are losing their way. And losing it in a big way. I am not going to go into your governments I been there, and it wasn't pretty. I will just say this. I saw a quote from your world very recently.

"While we have two hands, one to help yourself and one to help others."

Can I amend this quote Medium?

"You have two hands, two to help yourself."

It's not fair you think the way I see the human race. No?

**Author.** *No, I don't think it's not fair. I think it's deserved. In most cases its deserved.*

*Lightworkers. Most of us are here for to help others; we are waking up the world we have been given a job to do, if you don't like the way we do it change the title and add more jobs, with fractions and ways to work. Some are worth saving others are not so much not worth saving, but they are worth pointing in the right direction and shocking them awake.*

**Higher Guide.** Shocking them awake will not work Medium. They will explain it away.

**Author.** *Please tell me why the division is wider between the wakened and the sleepwalkers?*

**Higher Guide.** I know you see this happening day in and day out on your world. You are not given enough to work with. The consciousness of the human mind lacks stability, and the mental being is called into question.

**Et Guide:** Oh, do not like that name, and if you must and insist on naming me can you not give me a better one? (He wouldn't give me his name and was being a little rude.)

**Author:** *How about you describe yourself to me and il give you a name or you give me a Name.?*

**Dean:** I strongly dislike that name. And while your spirit guides do not mind what they are called and it's a just a label, it is for us too. Seeing as I am as yet the only off-world guide, or helper right now. I will give you my own name for this purpose, and you may use it or shorten it. I want us to work better together, I feel hostility.

**Author:** *No, I am not hostile I feel like you have made your mind up about the human race, without looking to all sectors of that race. Some of us are good well most of us are.*

**Dean:** Yes, I'm Thripedean that's the closest I can give you in your own language to my name, shorten it if you will, and It will be just.

**Author:** *Alright, then Dean. Does that work?*

**Dean:** (*Rolls his eyes*) And yes it works. Now work medium. We have much to do.

**Author:** *Nope let's just clear something up right now before we start.*

**Dean:** Rolls his eyes again.

**Author:** *Stop rolling your eyes at me and give me a break here. I have to work with you, and you I so let's just get on, do not treat me like a fool. While I might inhabit a body, right? And I might live on Earth; I am still a soul, what is it you said? A soul is a soul Right?*

*Then work right with respect like I Have given to you if you're having a bad day get over it and let's go. Please describe yourself for the readers. I will mention this again start from scratch.*

**Dean.** You are correct Medium I apologise; I have been interacting with your world for a long time and see nothing that interests me aside of the great divide, I do feel this can be changed to more to one side than the other. The racism the haves and have-nots vs the rich and the poor. Black lives matter alongside the women's movement, alongside the LGBTQ + communities.

The aids and HIV patient's vs the Cancer patient's vs other patients, we do not treat others like this in our world. We are all treated the same and maybe the sheer fact you have free will is causing this. Deportation and the splitting up of herds. No, I'm sorry families.

And many feel these rules or laws are best because they were made by who? I am sorry Medium I am struggling to come to terms with your Earth world. The energy is so much lower, the vibration the Spirit world work from is love and higher vibrational energy, they know we are harsher in energy and opinions we have no free will we do as we are told, this is your contract, and you follow it, but not all on our world are contracted. I am an energy traveller and high guide teacher and communicator. I move around the galaxies visiting other worlds and watching them, the souls I can't call them human they are not. But they are souls.

Souls from many worlds are contained far across the galaxy away from the Earth world they know of your existence down here. They know of your planetary systems and have worked with identifying many stars and stratospheric systems, they have worked with matter, but they see the damage done over aeons of time. The Dumping of space metal into the stratosphere. I do not come today to talk about your world our world is so much different.

I lived on the purple planet in the Galaxy of stebzoen (Closest). We are Billions of lightyears from your Earth world, but we travel through "time" to get to your world. We come through wormholes. Plural and while it's not yet available to measure this on your world you are so far behind other worlds. You make many discoveries, and we make more. CERN is as close to where we would expect your planet to be right now; you are still aeons behind us. I travel on the higher vibrational Quantum travel. Your world has seen us for a long time, there are "ones who dismiss us around your world", and ones who know we are here. We have to lower our vibrational energy like your loved ones to come to your world, but our methods of travel can do that easily and maintaining it is harder this is why we only visit for short periods of time.

We have been with your planet since the time of the great pyramids, they are significant for us. They are planetary in design. We cannot help those who will not help themselves we could make life on your planet so much easier was not allowed to interfere, but we can advise.

Your planet is moving into a higher vibration or a New Year, and as the divides get further apart the masses will move to the higher vibration, and the rest will be left behind, with tyranny.

I have often hoped this would shake these up. It's sadly not to be.

I give you measurements from your own world for my body.

I stand at eight feet-four inches Tall from feet to the top of my head. To the human Eye, I am as pleasing as you wish me to be. And realistically I am grey. Or classed as a grey but my skin is darker my eyes see better, and my circulatory system is better than that of the human, we are not what they have deciphered us to be, and we are connected to most on your planet. We are not savage we are here for helping you, we only ever help, but we do not see the human troubles as ours. We do not see trivialities as ours. We do know who a kind soul is, and who can work with us and who cannot.

Yes, Medium you argue back and as some do not like that, but a bit of fire makes work interesting, for though you answer back the spirit world think highly of your work, and I have been chosen to guide you through the rest of your incarnation then you return home with me. But I will help with your animal work and mediumship work your Dog work then you return to my world to continue your work with me. You will recognise me when you shed this body, but you saw me before in healing many years ago. Earth years.

**Author**. *Dean Why Now?*

**Dean**: Because your energy has called me called me back, to work with you again. To help teach others on your world to communicate this way.

**Author**: *Telepathic mind to mind.*

**Dean**: Yes, Medium they will know you. Many will remember you for this work and others, and the animals will flock, Jonathan was correct when the pieces come together your work will be busy.

**Author:** *Will I teach this to others?*

**Dean:** Yes, Medium the time is coming together you will be called to teach this. They will come in trickles we will be sending them, and now you have two channels you need a classroom full of them. But you will teach them right. And correct and I will guide you to help.

**Author:** *So why the hostility towards me?*

**Dean**. I do not care for your world, or the trivial lives led, they are souls having a human experience in a human body they are losing their way.

**Author.** *Tell me about the science in your world.*

**Dean.** I have been away from my world for a long time; my main living is the stratosphere above the earth world and the Spiritual world its self where I help teach channel and lower vibrational energy. Then moving souls up slowly until we are at the energetic channel level. They need to be able to compartmentalise the energy, and not many can do it.

**Author**. *How long have we worked together?*

**Dean.** Your world does not measure time as we do. We measure different, but regarding lifetimes compared to Earth I can say 60 Lifetimes. You came to incarnate to our world to measure levels in the air with a partner and the partner passed to the spiritual from our world you stayed. The measurements of time and energy-based foodstuffs for my people. Is what kept you in our world. Our world as my world is your world also.

**Author.** *Alright, I will leave this, so I now have a new guide is that my understanding here?*

**Dean.** Yes, I will follow through with night work.

See your much nicer to work with now.

**Dean**. (Smiling) Thank you now. Go. You have work to do medium.

**Author:** *We broke for the evening on this work and came back the next week, Gabe assisted this time.*

## Atoms and molecules DNA and genetic coding

**Dean:** Are seen in all the natural world each day from a leaf of a tree to the bark of a tree, to the dog hairs swept of floors; we leave DNA left behind the genetic coding of life. The Fibonacci spiral is coded in all of universal life, and life on other planets in other solar systems and universe parallel verses and multiverses. Life is in all things living on other planets in subterranean we grow most of the foodstuffs there, we live and survive well there.

Your own pyramids have a subterranean advantage over the upper-level inhabitants; there is no need for eyes in the mole, they have evolved that way, large teeth for chewing the roots and large claws for digging underground.

Otherworld inhabitants have a more substantial skull because the brain is so much larger than that of your world. The eyes are different because of the radial optic nerve we see different, we see mainly in four dimensions. We see at various angles; our hands are different because we use a totally different sensory system, the nerves carried from our spinal column are longer and more defined; we see through feelings and smells are not overly important, as we smell through the memory of seeing. Our reproductive systems are inside the body as our worlds are colder than yours. We live, within as our molecular systems much different but work very similar to yours.

We connect through the mind; much the same as many of your Mediums and telepathically through the mind into pictures the same as the discarnate soul. You come to our world to evolve the mind and lay down a structural core learning ability- and some of you carry this need and sponge-like memory to your own world through the soul memory.

Your world is a change to our own, not only is your energy and vibrational consciousness different, but they are poles apart. The intelligence of the human mind can be vast. The brain has not evolved to the capacity needed to work with minds like ours, this is why when we channel, the mind of the channelled will often leave with a headache, when learning, we very often do channel for learners of channelling.

I like the way its called channelling in your world, and communications in ours, as I'm talking to you now Medium. It's through the mind that's why this feels different from other channelled works, our world and your world is so much different, even if you only based them on this, we also know telekinesis is somewhat usual with us, and it's more than mind over matter it's a total sum of what is.

The Fibonacci sequence you see in your world is evident across the worlds. The DNA of life, the life force of the planetary systems is all still evolving they are evolving all the time.

While your NASA is looking for life on other planets they should be working on life under their own, there are no shortcuts to the pyramids; they were built by the pharaohs and many off world beings so many aeons ago. We also connected to them via the Energy circulating around the great pyramids, if you look at all of them built against the planetary system; you will notice there is a sequence of planets that mirror the graphical design of the Pyramids.

They are more than just tall man-made structures, that have been puzzling scientists for many years of your time. They cross on ley lines into Parallel times and through these times is where the structural differences will be found, the world is changing dimensional energy and vibration, and as this changes the pyramids will eventually give up the secrets she is buried from the eyes of the unworthy. The great shift has happened before 601 AD and will happen again. The empathic minds are feeling this shift. It's impossible for your World to see the overall results because you do not know what you look for, your way behind we are. We have tried to help we are turned away at every cause.

There is a shift and change and swap in your world leaders. We will not allow a nuclear war as it will impact more than your earth and your universe, these are egotistically minds at play. Though we will not allow this. We see many feel pushed into a corner because of this, the great migration of immigrants across your world like bison on the Serengeti they are not equipped to deal with the western world. No more than the western world is equipped to deal with their world. But you fail as a collective people, the hearts of the many are closed. And while many are awakened to the plight of the soul, many are prejudiced by the difficulties of the human body, the outside not the inside and while their cultures are different to your own, and somehow their savagery is also different but only as the selective, not a collective.

TAKE THEIR CULTURES AND WEIGH THEM AGAINST something you know, the breed standard of a dog. Everyone breeding said dog reads the breed standard differently.

Take their religious books, the Koran the bible the book of Jobe, the first testament, all books on your world and all about a "god" of such. All with rules and regulations and suitable only for the masses to be used against, because someone has read them different in the usual intentional way it was written.

I am going to bring this in again because it will mean something to someone. Take the Lord's prayer. Then take prayer from the Koran. Both of them are intended as good, but both of them are twisted to suit the twisted mind of the twisted who are reading it, I am allowed to call them twisted as I don't live in your spiritual world. I Live on my own, and we see the twisted that goes on, and we have dived into the mind of the good the bad and the downright ugly of your world.

Many of the souls on your world are using the "book" for their own end, to fuel hate. Did your gods not say suffer little children, is it not meaning all, as a collective or only a few. Just the few who perceive only a few to be worthy? Did he not say many other analogies, or are you only allowed to use ones that suit yourselves? Jesus lived a lifetime. Yes, he did.

YOUR GOD IS A FALSE PROPHET; FALSE PROPHETS ARE MADE by the people for the people.

In god, we trust, no in god only a few trusts because the god is being turned on by the people. So, let's go back, your god. Our god no.

No God. God is universal energy the divine the source of all things. When we return to the Divine, we return to source universal energy the total sum en mass of all things is energy and this is where you will return too. I reside in a better state of being that you are right now. The lessons around the lives you live are usually low learning lessons, and because we have no time in our world either we do not encroach you. We leave you be. We leave you to learn at your own pace with whoever you wish to learn with. The free will you all seem to have, that makes even the egotistical minds of the Earth world uninhabitable for us to wish to visit, its what is totally wrong with your world. While I am aware I sound to you Medium, I'm unimpressed with the behaviour on your world I am. Unimpressed.

But we have agreed from the beginning of time to help your world, your world leaders have turned us away, now we are at the point in your time we do not have the patience while governments half of them know we exist while other half is trying to believe we are invisible, we will only tolerate so much. We could just show ourselves if we requested to cause mass panic in your world we would, and it would be absolute we are not at that point yet. We are growing more intolerant of the "world leaders" only taking from us. It's not enough they have ruined or are ruining their own world they want to make it to other planets to "dig" there too. We will not allow it. I Will tell you now, many races live in your world as well as upon it. But you do not see. I leave that there now is not the time for this conversation Medium.

**Dean:** Tell me Medium to what end does it serve to touch another world, to what end?

You cannot move there, you have to find it first, and the $4^{th}$-dimensional vibrational energy is not able right now. Even the atmospheric conditions around your world are vibrating on the drag from the Earth world, at the same time the Gravitational pull around your $4^{th}$-dimensional world. Pull and suck the atmosphere around your world; so in and around for measured by space miles as I do not get your measurements. So space miles or our speed of light and sound is typical for our world no gravitational pull, this is only seen in the earth world as the total en mass of energy is off kilter so tell me Medium why do they look for life on other planets? They have to navigate through the space dump they have around your world first, and we expect them for us to let them do this to other worlds. As you would say, and I know this I watch you enough. "not bloody likely".

Your world needs to be filtered out; we understand the lettuce idea, of planting lettuces at alternate days to have a crop all the time, your spiritual world needs to implement this with souls who chose bodies that implicate others who are on the right path, as many of you are.

Now I have picked your governments apart it's obvious we are not impressed, but this is not just the USA president you have now. I Could go back to Nixon and before him to pick at your world. We use this as an example but go to Germany to Poland where the LGBTQ are slaughtered where the white skinned people are fighting for rights. This is a divide and conquers world not bringing them together world.

In Japan, high in the mountains, there is an animal that lives solitary lifestyle who come together one to mate and then raises families, and this is ingrained to the core memory of the soul to procreate and not to learn other ways. No, bring them together, and you have a mass of souls who do not have any connections to each other. And while this is an example and alright, take that analogy to the western world and spread it around a little. Add a politician into the middle of it shouting against equal rights for all, and one to divide and conquer as individuals this is where the lightworkers of your world are at. You can wake people one at a time, and the issues around that you are stuck for others like you to talk and interact with, so you all prefer your own company. Then take the procreate, and you're the animals high in the mountains of Japan.

Working as a collective to expand the awakened and connections to the soul, are what you are there for. So many are rushing into the life they are notable for and falling flat and burn, and so many are not living in their own truth. Because of what the politician in the middle is doing, the politician is using your vote to big themselves up enough to not make an impact on your lives. But to continue to divide and conquer, the point of this whole mass here is to act as a collective and join together, use this incarnation to do better than before, to move the incarnated world forward into that higher dimensional frequency.

For the only mass soul, energy will bring about a change of the energy around the natural world. The DNA of the Earth world is changing all the time so make sure you leave good footprints not bad ones, stop the Man in the middle the "politician" dividing and conquering for it's not his job.

I wish you a good day, and thank you medium for working with me today, you confound us all with the ability to just pick us up energy based, and I will work with you again soon.

***Author.*** *"This was one of Deans Harder channels the first one I did with him. His POV of our world from his vantage point. It wasn't a good POV that I'm positive about."*

*"Keeping with the Off-world guides I bring another in here before I bring Dean back. We had no name."*

**"Medium F Was assisting with this work and channel."**

**MF:** "As we move forward with our work today, I want to have you welcome in the soul giving you that niggly headache. He doesn't wish to give you a name as yet, so l step aside Author, and here he comes."

**Off-world Guide:** "Good evening Author as we work, I need you to realise by not allowing names into your book you have given so many more of us a platform to speak freely and much we have is controversial as well you know. Much needs to be said. And less is allowed at this time in history."

"I can hammer home all that's been said but it is boring as you know, so let me give you this, from here on in all is new to you."

"In the beginning when we allowed the prophesiers to see into the future of what the earth world and others would be like, they were given free rein as it were. And of course, looking back through history books, things like vampires and werewolves where found to be fabled and made up. Though the minds and tracking them rumours and stories are hard to find because many of the "made-up" stories were in fact not made up. Vampires and were-wolves were and had been known as many other things, and ones we will not waste your time going over. And again your world has had many a fabled history, regarding the made-up children's story or how the world came to be, one, in fact, your scientists seem to have more input than the story of the "bible" maybe the seventh-day man needed a rest.

WASN'T AS MADE UP AS IT SEEMS FOR WE DID, IN FACT, NEED a rest. It took some of the greatest species there long enough to repopulate a planet. The ecosystem then was suited to the inhabitants, and flora and fauna now are not as suited, so if you go back over all the species and sub-species inhabiting your earth world today, this is why so many insects and birdlife have gone extinct. There have been extinctions of animals and sea life that your human scientists have not known to document because they didn't know they existed in the first place. Amongst these extinc-tions have been the plants that would have could have provided the medicine basis for many of the man-made illnesses you have today.

The crop spraying of all chemicals into the earth's atmosphere is poisoning your world. Now I understand many will fail to see this has anything to do with what we are talking about, because why do you even need the plants if they are killing them, I will tell you again this comes back to greed. In as we can only hammer home so many times your companies that make medicines to treat the ills of your world are killing you all. There is very little I can say on that, and I do not wish to waste time going over it. So, I leave that and go back."

"When the earth world was created, we needed to house a soul. A soul we had helped develop a core learning into. This soul needed a vehicle, a body housing, and this body needed to be suitable for the earth we created. And we built this body or engineered it based on the world you would live in, you see we had a time-frame we knew by our brightest scientists that the world would evolve. And we needed a body that could also evolve, however, the core structural DNA needed to be able to evolve and this is where we came to an improvident problem. The DNA would need to not only affect the brain and evolve the body, but we couldn't not together. Let's just say we could do what we needed only in the timeframe we were given, ecological wise. Not biological wise."

"The brain would be needed to grow and learn and pass down, ideologies of the world in which you lived; come on we struggled with bringing people into an ice age and have them not look like the animal. To house a very intelligent soul we needed a brain that could master simple structural lessons, this, of course, we found limited over aeons of time. The ego that came with the human wasn't intentional, but free will was. We never expected the human to be so diverse, but the soul we did. It wasn't that we messed up. It was we couldn't form the fractions of the body to evolve to the higher diverse brain intelligence and be on parallel to the soul intelligence, and so it fell short, so you fall short as human, nothing coincides. This would answer the question of why people can look the same but be so different in ideals and intelligence. Mathematicians awakened the parts of the brain we hoped would awaken for "normal intelligence" it never and the scientist's brain awakened the soul core intelligence bringing what we had hoped for, into line for all. We fell short. So, using these we designed the DNA structural core for body choices in the spiritual world, there is a body choice for an intelligence choice if decided upon for soul lessons. I am explaining it as simple as I can for the human brain of the majority that will read this book; your own guide Author has stated it needs to be understood by the majority, not just a few."

**Off world guide:** Now the terms and conditions of Autism and Asperger's and singleton brain structures that bring these into the fore for many. The most highly intelligent souls on your world find themselves; in a body that is structurally slower than that of the scientists. For the simple reason, the DNA doesn't match the intelligence by the family trait. *Autism appears to be across the universe in all they deem not "Normal" They are so highly developed Man needs an excuse to isolate them. So many diverse "symptoms" they barrier them under one label.*

On the off chance, we have a DNA match that can crop up once or twice, we add that to the soul's choice via contract. So now we move on, the grey, for example, the body is designed with the brain as so advanced the body doesn't need to be as such. I am not going to give away the details of breeding upon their world I'm not going to give details like this into a spiritual book, though I'm sure your author has these details from her work with the greys of old.

MANY OF THEIR BODY IDEALS ARE DESIGNED AS NEED. EYES are very similar to that of spiders the way they see in sections seeing sparks an image in the brain sent to the optical nerve, and this is the main process. That said they eyesight of the grey changes from birth to adolescent and then again of the worker and the soldier, and the hierarchy is different to that of the human, all working for a common goal, family structures are very different. Young ones are reared together in a type of commune with parental roles while the parents are working. The whole family system is different compared to humans and other planetary species." *(Another Grey guide will work with you for this)*

"Each planet has their own sub-families if you can call them that, they are raised totally different. Working with the greys you will know that compared to other planets they are of higher intelligence, and the human and Orion based planets are going to make them appear hard to live and communicate with, therefore isolating them as a being will never work. They are spiritual race and have a deeper-rooted understanding of other planetary beings than that of Orion's inhabitants. Orion's belt is what your humans know this planet as, but the inhabitants are a reptilian based being and are much more subservient than many of the beings in nearby planets.

They are often misunderstood because of their appearance, but as I said the planet is a water-based planet, and reptilian beings are much suited, though do not misunderstand them as being stupid or sub as they are far from it, their brain capability far outweighs that of the human being and that of the harsher beings. While they are not overly spiritual, they understand the need for a free will in the human race, and while their planet it behind in technological capabilities, to that of the greys they work together with them, though they disagree the need to have a political system, like that of other planets."

"The planetary coalition that dictates the comings and goings of other planets and beings from world to world and they look after only the planets in the solar systems around the galaxy in which the earth is situated. Aucturians are extremely spiritual but also highly technological; they are next to the greys often mistaken for being the same though similar in outward visually the colour of their skin often depends on the light in which they are seen, they are also a telepathic race, along with them and greys. And many others these beings are beings of light and often seen within the counsel of twelve. Though these are not as often channelled as your humans would like to believe.

Humans have made a mockery of the twelve and are not amused, but they understand that other races are often the culprits for these mistakes, with the human race and often are only channelled when passed from the spiritual to the council. Thus, a spiritual guide from the spiritual world will introduce the soul from the human world to channel the twelve. Many don't take them as seriously as they would like because of this. Many metaphysical jokers are making them appear as they are being channelled please human/medium be careful whom you listen to if it appears odd/off and too farfetched it usually is.

The saying that annoys our Author and others is "Dear one", and this is earth saying not a channelled saying, I believe I'm being corrected here. Your Archangel Michael has said it once or twice, it's not an Off world common saying, that is what I should have said. I apologise.

When they begin with this you have a good idea there is no channel involved. I am trying and failing to make you see sense, and channelling from the spiritual is the only way I can do this; your own guide **Johan** allows me through, to do this along with the mediums of the spiritual world in which you work."

"Lemira is the name of a crystal the Lemurian seed, a powerful stone it is so used correctly, we are the people also from a time in the crystal city. We have inhabited your world. We have helped build your ecosystem we are a long way from our original home on the way to other planets and are channelling alongside the spiritual world, for we need to help with this book, that their Author is writing on their behalf. Lemurian peoples are not seen by the human eye as we are only seen from the parallels it is, we are vibrationally higher than the eye can see.

THE CHANNELLING TAKES MORE OUT OF US THAN THE earth human body, as you allow your vibrational energy to be able to connect to us, we tend to give the feeling of sickness, please it's not that you are, it's an energy source you're working with. We often assist in medical issues around your world with the higher guides. What will work and what won't, now we are on our way to your Red Planet in the galaxy you Author have been too. And no we can't just get there like the spiritual beings of light can we have to get there, the way your peoples would take into space, only our vehicle is much more of our own making than yours. Our metals are not metals at all."

**Author:** "*Why call them that?*"

**Off-world Guide:** "It's how I can make you understand is to show you. You will struggle to understand with the puny human brain; I am not insulting your intelligence medium/Author I know this is beyond your capability or range of knowledge. You are an intelligent being coming from your world. You do not have a point of reference to work with so watch Author and il show you."

**Off-world Guide:** "Remember the film in the 1980s flight of the navigator the metal of their transport is like this is shimmers and disappears and reappears but doesn't go invisible it's just the human eye can't see it as the vibrational vision we would see. It appears as a haze as it comes into being and goes again. Bright silver in appearance for the flickering I can see. I am not allowed to show you Author the inside of our transport I can at a later date for later channels but not, yet I'm limited right now. We will arrive at the Red planet within the "earthly timeframe of one month. Now the vampires and werewolves were started somewhere as for where the Alien life forces. We were in touch with your planetary higher forces long before you "seen us" only the capture of other lifeforms have caused many troubling issues with many races as your underground science labs have "made" aliens.

And fed the rumours of the greys, they have laid

down carefully planned whistle-blowers. Many of the people who are living with the worry of being whistle-blowers have been set up. Set up to blow the whistle. They know the earth people are so egotistical in their thinking that they lead them to believe we are only the one species in the whole of the galaxies. Author your world is far more damaging than all the worlds in all the star systems and the level of conspiracy is frightening, even to the off-world inhabitants like us, we worry for your world.

Your scientists are cloning clones of us. Using DNA from Rosewell, they make human-made Aliens. I will not even give them credit and call them higher beings they are not. Souls are all souls differing only in energy and vibrational changes. No matter the planets they inhabit. This channel is one of the few that will work with Higher beings of light. Off-world beings are coming to the Earth to guide the few into a higher vibrational being as per soul contract."

"Author this is where we say goodbye for now. We will meet again. You now know my energy and il give you my name next time we meet. Good day to you Author."

***AUTHOR:*** *"ALL IN ALL, IT'S BLATANTLY OBVIOUS WE ARE not alone;"*

*"We come to a fun part of the book; I met with a couple of Earth regressionists and a Medium who had passed to spirit a few years before. Much like the Regressionists and yet it was a fun days channelling. I named this channel the regressionists shock as we go off world, there are multiple guides and Guardians in this channel I'm not changing it up so please sit tight it's very interesting. It amused me a lot. The intelligence of spirit."*

## 2

## GABE CAME IN TO WORK WITH, BUT DEAN WAS STILL IN THE BACKGROUND

**Author:** *What the intention of working with other planetary souls? Like the greys, I see they have a bad reputation here on earth.*

**Gabe:** The reputation comes from many films and not knowing. We too do not have a good reputation; I also see that your question comes from an article you have just read today. The intention comes to show the souls incarnating on the Earth world right now, that another life exists outside of their planetary systems. We wouldn't have allowed the interaction between yourself, Dean unless it was a genuine one, we have you well protected as well as your protection when working. We need the souls incarnated to realise that the world is not what they perceive it to be. The Matrix of the spiritual world rumour is a way of blocking and controlling that feeling of being out of control and feeling nothing can be done to help; it causes humans actually to fear death.

Death holds no fear, the fear of "going to hell" comes from the Religious belief. Again, if you fear "hell" then maybe you have done something in the lifetime to cause this fear of judgement.

"Hell" is again based on the religious belief of the soul the same as "heaven" is a religious belief of the soul. The Spiritual world is a "heaven" if you like. So, if your belief is Heaven/spiritual world at the point of physical death, your transition to the spiritual world is one of the same. And a surprising journey to the Religious soul.

So, the Greys and the Reincarnation Matrix is a fear-based idea painted into the brain of the human by Others who have maybe Heard this, read about this and or channelled something they shouldn't have.

Channelling was very popular once upon a time, within the spiritual communities. There are in fact very few Real Channels alive/Incarnated right now. For this reasoning alone is an explanation. Many persons sitting down to work with our world, have no known preconceived ideas that they could be channelling just "anyone". Working with the other world the intention comes from love, yes but you might also get a "slipped in" soul. A soul intent only from working from the other side, this other side the lower consciousness soul. The lower Consciousness soul and we have used this term countless times throughout the work we do with you.

We mean, and you know it that it's the lower energy, or the soul coming in from a not so good space. And while we work with these souls, they are still contactable via a detrimental energy channelling; This is where the groups of negative souls you reap what you sow, you have heard that. I do not want to tell you there is a hell because I would be leading you wrong. So, let's explain it like this.

When you transition from your world to ours and your religion expects you to be in hell, and you do too because of something is done in the lifetime. It makes you afraid of death.

You die, and you come to a part of our world where all the souls on the same energy level as yourself go to, the lower level lower consciousness.

Lower Energy, this is the Level of our world you come to, you will reside here. Souls based on the physical plane your world can channel these souls in the lower levels, not coming from a space of love. This is where a lot of the "grey" information comes. We have blocked these sorts of communications of late. However, some still get through. It's because of this we are teaching "relatives of loved ones" to Channel. We aim to have at least one or two channels in each soul group; it's a mass undertaking, and it's been going for such a long time "years by Earth standard" as we know time is not measured here. I know as a Time Measuring planet it's hard for you to see our "days" and "Nights" it's Eternally light here a light that's consuming in love and energy for the light beings who reside here.

I see this "Grey" issue bothered you. Our Work with the higher guides for progress for us and us for them, we teach humility we teach love, and we teach more "emotions" as the worlds they inhabited are not emotional realms, many of their souls incarnate into the Earth world also learning the same as Souls from here do. Many of their Souls are the third wave of souls or the souls who cannot lie. The souls who will not have children who will not be caught up in the Karma of the physical Earth world. They are the spiritual teachers of your world they are the teachers of other planets. Many collective consciousness souls or the new soul into mass Lessons are souls from other worlds for they are brave souls.

I am not saying our souls are not either; I say many of

the souls in the third wave are from outer planets. They incarnate and vibrate at another energy, they are sensitive souls they are the star seed souls, they take up the cause for many of the souls coming in direct from the spiritual world. They are leading the way.

**Author:** *Can I ask about the Water found on Mars? I know from the work we do here that they live subterranean will the Human ever see them? Do they want to be discovered?*

**Gabe:** Ah Not me you should be speaking to he is coming.

**Dean:** When we spoke the last time, I said we would not allow your Earth people to dig on other planets. We have been avoiding your Astronauts; its highly preferential the other world is not discovered; the subterranean grounds are well developed and highly inhabitable we do not concern ourselves with the goings on of the human who wishes to bring untold damage to other worlds when they damage the world they inhabit. Now we are not easily concerned by their efforts to know that anything they find we allow them to see.

My "people" for want of a better word, are far superior to the planets we inhabit.

While working with you last week, I realised that though I do not wish to have to deal with the Emotional side of the human, agreeing to work with you, puts me on the direct path. You're not emotional I am not saying that. I'm saying you called me out on my shit and I apologise. I should be able to adjust to the species I'm working with this is my "ability" this is why it's me. I also didn't expect you to call me out on my bad attitude to your questions as we worked.

Know we have to work on a book together, so I know I have the learn to be more tolerable. I work with other species, not Human, and the souls are not bound by free will either and put up with me, I get used to it.

Our species are far more intelligent, and human "feelings" are not bound to us.

**Author.** *Are you saying the feelings we have as human are only seen in the Earth world inhabitants, and not across the Multiverses?*

**Dean:** Yes, that is exactly what I am saying. Your world is the harshest to live on, and that is solely caused by free will. It gets the Human into trouble. They have learnt to be devious and misconstrued; they have learnt to be Egotistical and spiteful towards their kind. They have a range of emotions our Outer world species do not have. Or have to deal with. It's hard to get used to. Though you are a good human.

**Author** *Thank you for a compliment I'm delighted.*

**Dean.** They have learnt Sarcasm.

**Author:** *Dean can you tell me about the role you play in Your world, what is your job?*

**Dean:** My job if that's what you call it, is to travel as communication across the universe yours and others to extend the hand of peace, and to show other species we are not the "Evil Alien" we have been made out to be. I am to show that spiritual beings are more than just from the worlds you know. I am to show that we work based on Love. Also, we do not have many Emotions in our species, but Love is one we do have. Its Love for ourselves and others that push us to teach our young ones to help across the planetary systems and show that the "Greys" are not the bad guy.

To teach someone to be afraid of you is to show them the wrong side to you. We have been involved in Human experiments of old. And we have I do not deny this. Trials across the multiverse and the galaxies yours and others. Our Species have also been involved in "experiments" by other planets. It's how we learn from each other.

When the Earth world was developed, your world had to be inhabited, you have worked with Johan and Jacob, regarding developing Eco-systems on other planets Yes?

**Author:** *Yes. We worked about the animal and the Spiritual Worlds Red planet and others yes.*

**Dean:** then you know that the Ecosystems are built. First, this takes many aeons. Then the inhabitants the food chains and so on. Then the "human body" was developed for the planet. The Neanderthals homo-sapiens Early Man Many more early developments of man. These were developed in our experiments across the Worlds and the Ecosystems Humans where developed for the use of the soul to experience life. The Earth collective soul system worked with the Early Man. As man Taught themselves consciousness developed. All were helped by "Aliens, It's" My Species. Man is now ahead of their brain; their brains are underdeveloped, and the upgrades needed to keep them with the rest of the planets are not available. They must continue to apply the learn and grow and Evolve techniques. The Early connections to the spiritual world and our world were coming from this Early in Mans development. We never mind that Man has got ahead of themselves on what they developed over what was already in place, we do not have the Jealousy or the emotions around the blame game as the Earth world does. They complain about simple things they complain about stupid things. And yet take them from their comfort zone and talk about death and it's evident that they are not as evolved. This is my Job to Help teach across the Seven Worlds.

**Author:** *Dean is there Seven worlds or Seven Specific Worlds?*

**Dean**: I knew you wouldn't let that slide. There are Seven, Physical Worlds vibrating at similar levels. A world within a world if you like, the Parallel worlds alongside the mental world. The Consciousness worlds that the consciousness grows and becomes aware of the vibrational differences between these worlds. Animal Worlds. There are Water worlds. Adage worlds where species that have become extinct in your world are living. Worlds within a world. It's my Job again I am limited if it was just telling you, but this is for your book. I Will work with you still on the other book so yes more work and more information I can give.

The scientific minds of your world will be better suited to any of the other planets. These other planets have incarnated souls gleaning many decent lessons and memories upon these different worlds and all line up entirely within the solar system around your world. Your Author of books channelled with characters has many characters coming from these worlds. "Men" of other species not unlike your own the basic Biology is there with some noticeable differences. Differences needed for the worlds they inhabit. And many of them are dotted across the seven planets.

**Author.** *Why Now or have We been biding our time?*

**Dean:** Each soul is different; every soul is born with an Affinity for certain abilities. When we see these abilities show in the soul at birth. We are notified to see if the soul is a precise "fit" if you like the work we are doing.

Your soul was the perfect fit. As your mind is asking me is there no one else?

Well no. Your work with channelling and Animals makes your mind and consciousness the right fit for this job, and others sent to you to do similar work will find that their thoughts are similar on the electromagnetic impulse scale as your own with their Affinity to individual abilities. We know you are not "Ego-based, you simply do not care" but not caring is not a wrong way, not caring what other souls think of your path, and knowing that path does the work we ask of you easy. This will be your hardest job. Teaching others to have Faith in their work.

First, you need to teach to work with their team; I know you do this. But knowing you came not alone you're just the front man if you like, is enough to kill the Ego of anyone. Taking credit for a team's work a lot of souls wouldn't dream of it. If they could see their team. Not seeing the team and knowing you're working in a team is hard for some newly Earthly developed lightworkers/mediums. This is what you have to teach. To thank their team. For if they can grasp this, then the Ego merely drops because they will never dream of taking credit in a team, they will take credit for the whole team, but the guides don't wish this. The guides then spin it to tell them, if they don't believe in their work then find the guide will not steer them wrong. Believe to have faith. If they can't do this, then they are in the wrong profession. You would never think of telling someone well I don't believe I'm right, but they told me to say to you. It's not done I have seen the way some of your Earthly teachers teach Mediumship, and they steer to many wrongs.

**Dean:** We have been watching progress made in a very small teaching group yourself, and three others have been working with for over a year. You wrapped up before your Human Holiday.

Your teacher will be introduced to more "Aliens" over the next year to sixteen months. Then one other person left. And left three including you as strange as this seems we have been watching and waiting for three Earthly years. We know that this sounds odd to you and will to others, in total forty-six years of watching, three of them waiting. It's a long time, and yet when I am told I have to work with a soul, I look and watch and see who it is I have to work with before that. I will not step in until I know this soul is not at all strange or feels strange to be working on a telepathic level with an outer being or other world soul or E.T soul.

When you are comfortable and can believe that I am in fact "real" And do not concern yourself with opinions of others, then I stepped forward, with the help of your Medium friend in the spiritual world. I almost said guide, but we know he is not your guide or anyone's incarnated, he is just helping for the book from his experience. When he brought you to me, and almost blew your head off, he took a step I never expected, and I dare I said it neither did you. The Higher consciousness energy was so intense, that headache cleared faster than I expected with you. I knew they were correct in the assumptions why you?

Mediumship is Evolving you have said this often, and yes this is true. Your teacher also feels this. And you must Evolve with the movement or risk left behind. Now that said the consciousness of the planets lightworkers are struggling and opting for a safe option. What will happen is rather than bring their students forward they will get them to a point and unable to move past this point because of limitations on their developments. They need to learn to channel the higher guides and ask for directional learning. This they can take to their classrooms. We see you take the course you were well able for along with your friends. Yes, friend's lifelong friendships and working partnerships come from development like that. You will take this into Animal work and soul work rather than Directional mediumship.

Directional Mediumship from my standpoint and what We call Mediums who are moving and developing into a specific area of Mediumship, but they are directed from the higher realms. I heard that thought in your mind forming as I was speaking to you Author. It's not a new term for my world; it is a relatively new term for yours.

Now to answer the question then we will wrap this up for this evening. As your Energy is flagging, and yes well done. Iron and nuts.

To answer why me why now? Have we been biding our time?

Now the Earth world has evolved into realising there is life on other planets. We have been lining this work up with you. For the past forty-six human Earth years. Life lessons and development in the dream state channelling, and learning to regulate the temperature of the guides around you. Via Energy directional work comes from the higher sources when working so working with this energy. Helps us to use your skill set to bring in our conscious minds. The conscious mind of the human is bored of boring "human" stuff if you like, the world of spirit is presented by many in black and white.

They still twist and turn to make it hard for the ones coming behind. We also are needing the other worlds consciousness represented. We have been biding our time but only because certain channels and guides are developing together. There are a few students headed your way. And one of these is known to you, your guides have the same name, and you worked with her before.

This student is a channel for them, the conscious mind is being strengthened by the spirit to move into the higher realms and as you know this can take a while depending on your final path. Some guides will come with the image of them, not the same as who they are; the will present to the Psychic painter/Artist as "different" In the mind's eye as they are. As she realises this, she can ask them to show the true form. And yes, they will like I did for you and then transformed back to the "more eye-pleasing" not because we are ashamed of our more Spiritual look, but because clairvoyant mediums are sometimes put off channelling by something that might trigger a response in the human part of the brain. And though you are a soul, the human element will kick in. This is why I prefer telepathic linking into the Human mind.

And author I will work with you tomorrow.

**Author:** *This finished our channel With Dean and Gabe took over a week apart.*

# 3

# TWO REGRESSIONISTS, AND AN ALIEN

**Author**: *"Morning NM &CD how are you this fine morning?"*

**NM**: "Are you sarcastic Author, we heard you chatting this morning your time (He winks) and decided it's time. Metaphorically of course.

**Author:** *"I know there is no time in your world, what's with the time jokes?*

**NM: "**Just having fun Author. Let's begin, again in your world I must tell you there was many more than the 7k documented works, only that many were used for the LBL work. I sat at my desk glasses down my nose with an old cassette recorder and an old Dictaphone; there was also the written notes. I didn't want to miss anything, and yet I used this for my backup work. Many have documented I said this I said that and who knows maybe I did, please Author take it with a pinch of salt the documented work the earthwork is way behind the work I'm doing here.

You, of course, didn't expect me to arrive in fine form and do nothing?

Yes, Author, my own forefinger was annoying me with

arthritis down to years of writing, and a little bit banged up, I ask you to take your time and get us as both of us want to come in this morning with you, come on in D.

**CD:** "Why thank you for allowing us time to speak with you, I know you're busy and want to get on but your good also at putting off work. I know you have been rather confused as the what is happening. And you got some direction this morning, please the way you said it is correct, animals and god and yet I Feel Dean might be best suited to here; the higher guides and off-world guides are so apt in our past. I know that the people NM worked with had little to no connection, older earth souls not older world planet souls. And that stunted work and yet we both see now, that moving to Europe as in my own work, we have a variety of people, of humans. (*Pronounced u-mans*) Many where of off-world it helped too for the ET work I was doing. I had near enough clarification, and yet spirit didn't put this into the path of NM for him to work with, he needed just immediate. It was groundbreaking, but as much as we have been called all sorts of crackpot names, it's correct the work would have been dumbed down if the off-world planetary people would have been remembered by many. And yet some documented cases where but not enough for him to say right we have a race of off-world people or another species."

**CD stands back, and NM comes forward,**

**NM:** "Author you have to understand Ets wasn't on the radar, and yet we were getting them from the memories of the many, we weren't working on them. And yet I have them filed away, I know they are known of, but it was too groundbreaking my work would have been discontinued, as it was the funding given-was working well."

"I Suppose I'm just here today Author, to ask you to mention there is a moving point on my work. It was only ever meant as a yardstick, more cases there are many more LBL Regressionists Author, many more will have found out what I had and moved the yardstick again, we trained a lot to do this work, one of them my friend. Did you see the memorial they done for me Author?"

**Author:** *"I'm not sure I did I seen something where someone was speaking, I never stayed up to watch it no. NM"*

**NM:** "Well it was a beautiful gesture and yet not needed I'm here now and having fun with the work with the younger mediums of the calibre."

**Author:** *"Can I Ask you a question?"*

*"The waking to consciousness from the planetary system you're from, that is correct isn't it, I been working online with this theory."*

**NM:** "I have someone who can talk to you about that, and yes it's correct now here he comes he wants to be called he, and you know him, Author."

## Awakening your soul to your home planetary system via the superconscious memory.

**Shaibi:** "No we have never worked together before, NM and yet we have so I leave this here for now. Author your recent work with the consciousness or the planetary system, in which you incarnate from, is the minimum beginning of awakened consciousness. So many souls are awakened higher from the get-go of their spiritual journey depending on soul contracts of when this shift will happen in their lives, reason many star seeds soul contracts are slightly harder than the average souls. You tend to take on too much, you have always been the same, and yet this is not altogether a good thing or a bad thing. And we know from the beginning of your incarnated earth times, because you are from the none free will world, the free-will upon the earth world catches many out straight away into the karmic lifetimes after that. And yet you still all keep coming, I'm not talking about you as per say Author from the outset, your karmic lives are done. This is an exceptional lifetime you have taken on; Author I am talking about other star seed souls.

Many think Earth is an easy planet, oh how wrong they all were and let you know each other, you're drawn by the vibes you emanate towards each other, you are drawn towards each other in the lifetime. Just as Spiritual people know their own. Please know as your all from different star systems throughout the galaxy and beyond, you are awakened to that higher consciousness. And much of the human biological body cannot take this energy. And many illnesses are caused, much like overcharged I would say, it's a simple analysis but hard to put right, we take you back to the spiritual world each night-time. Energy is meant to be cleared left from these connections into the earth world daily. Clear this person, or you may find your energy centres out of sync

Author-it doesn't matter where you're from, or where you originate. You go back to the spiritual world each night through dream-space but you know this, you all know this if you have read Authors work you know about the dream-space."

## Each soul has one Contract, per body.

Your home in spirit, you're in your soul colours, you see your own soul brothers and sisters your own level of the group by the colours, and yet you all look the same to your own eyes, for example. Author Pale blue is that of your Ascended Master, and yet only you see them as pale blue, for the same soul group all see him as pale blue. And he sees you like the same colour, vibrating from on his vibrational consciousness wavelength, your own group of souls your own wavelength learn together, and yet not all are pale blue, each Ascended Master has his own colour for teaching. Let's say this your Ascended Master Author is pale blue; and your working on higher connections to the galaxy over from our own, its Multiverse Piryon, (And no author not the character the planet, not known from your own world,) you're working there with your own soul groups. We are attempting connections to this planetary system as we move through the planets and other worlds as we gain a higher connection, we are able to skim through the spiritual worlds and by-pass the animal worlds.

Each soul group from the spiritual world have lessons classrooms in which they learn, and now we will bring in soul ***LH***. She would be known to you in your circle of friends, and she too is star-seed with a guides name the same as yours. She is pale yellow in the colour you see her soul robes and soul colour, in the spiritual world they colour by soul robes, or light-bodied, both of you are on the higher system of souls and yet the connections you both hold slightly vary, in some aspects and vastly in others. And you both connect to each other and work within the higher stations here in the spiritual world. Spiritual teachers of the world, it's hard to hear is it not author that your soul is just that little older than you anticipated. You are incarnating to help with the path your TF suggested to you recently and to learn patience which you have very little off, and now we move to another soul in your circle though she too is further on than most she is a good 1536 earth years behind you and ***LH***. And that is not too far she is learning her soul group colour is pale green. The healing colour right now. Healer and medium of the life. And these are too the animal people; they work with animals. Do not discount them by the colour of their souls; Author many of them have more than one job upon the earth world, many are interested in many things. Very few of that soul group do not meet up with their partners in life for a few Earth years yet. They are the middle group to the three of you in that group of friends, and though behind you in this she is too star seed. I do not know where that term was coined but we like it, and many of us still use this for the Earth people who channel here and yet where is here Author?

**Shaibi:** I am here in the spiritual world in the halls of learning, in the revolving world room, look around Author, look around and do you recognise, (He points to three Archangels standing there, and it's a memory) Do you see?

**Author:** *Yes, I do.*

**Shaibi:** In preparation for your coming here, into this room nearly four early years ago when your first meditation involving them happened in Belfast am I right?

**Author***: Yes, you're correct.*

**Shaibi:** Michael, Raphael, and Gabriel. And there you have it, your protection, your healer, and your Communicator. And your screen of the seven worlds and universes, we couldn't show it to you all Author, not back then. Now see the smaller planets and that smaller blue on. That's home Author. My home your home and ***Rhaji's*** home. Home is where the soul is, and yet you're not anchored there, you're anchored into the spiritual world; as that was part of the agreement by the galactic twelve when we were allowed to come many aeons of time. The twelve are not twelve higher beings the twelve are twelve planets taking part in populating the Earth, one representation of each planet. As an Elder Author your abilities where needed, along with many others, our planet is older than earth world Author by a lot. I can't say we are older by twelve, we are much older we were with the team while populating and setting the eco-system, now I was working with ***Jacob*** at the time and other souls, you were working on the animal planets; helping and training for many lives looking after animals.

**Author**: *This is interesting.*

**Shaibi:** Yes, but not really getting us anywhere.

**Author**: *No not really but it's still interesting, can you give me something on soul colours, more than that and by the twelve. The twelve planets agreed to incarnate with the Earth souls or the spiritual world souls destined for the earth?*

*Also, can you give me which souls are older by the energy the spiritual world or the Star seed souls?*

**Shaibi:** Firstly, Author And yes, why not? I will give you this and then we must get on, I'm trying hard to accommodate your energy this day, its super higher than yesterday, the Earth world energy hangs around the soul when your channelling and the headache you feel or felt yesterday, was the body trying to interrupt the connection. As you can see your guides accompany us today along with ***NM, CD. BSs.*** Twelve planets yes agreed to allow souls to come help populate the earth, it was a new planet and a new project overseen by the elders of the spiritual world. We needed older souls from each planet or scientists as your world calls them to help build the ecosystem, ***Dean*** was one of them too you know him, he was working on irrigation and other waterways. ***Jacob*** assisted with fauna and flora, you all had jobs to do, and all animals soul came from across the universes and galaxies. Many we had to engineer on other planets, there needed to be a footprint back to the beginning of time for the Earth people to find.

The planet has timelines each new planet has a timeline, a beginning a blueprint if you like. Biodiversity counts for a lot; many organisms would need to be left as a footprint for the scientists of the future to find the ways of timing or registering age. And many of you on that programme wanted to help bring the planet into fruition, so many of you have many lifetimes upon that planet- and various lifetime on other planets. Always considering the timeline of the planet earth, you knew that free will would cause many issues with the humans of the world. And yet you stayed. Now going back only one-hundred earth years ago; the call across the universes went out to the twelve involved, to call to action a task force to help bring the human souls into the truth of their age. The negativity around the planet was the cause of many effects. However, we fight a bigger problem that is truly over lies; we fight consciousness waking people up. However, the killing of their own people the governmental resources being used against.

I could talk a lot, but I won't so we move on. The twelve intervened again and said that only those involved in the birth of the planet- should be the ones going to help out. And yet the contracts were set in motion Author it's taken a long time, there are not enough words in the Your Tongue to hold that conversation. With people, we are better showing them when they come home each evening. Many spiritual world souls versus the twelve planets souls, where called together it had to be this way, as many souls from the twelve would help raise the consciousness of the spiritual world souls. And as it is you are having some struggles as its only becoming aware recently despite the past one-hundred earth years' timelines, that this even exists, the forefathers were shot down as mentally deranged, there are no Alien outside forces. There is no awakening, the list goes on, and yet the lower energies are sitting in your governments; and only when the people wake to the truth and topple the governments will change come on your earth world.

It's happening Author the younger generations are going to be the change, and for the next two more generations- they will fight to see the many continents; of your world change. Your work in your own contract will change the minds of the many when they start to wake up.

Your next part I ran over there didn't I, soul colours. Pale silver is our higher souls in the world in which you come from Author. Next, we have a mix of pale blue and golden yellow they are above the pale blues, but of course, it really doesn't make much difference. So, we go to the planets of the friends we spoke of last night, will we? Pale green is a ways from the top of the soul incarnations for that planet, but also the top of the line for the animal areas of that planet, a top healer colour should I say. Though the planet came into the twelve last and as relatively young star system by your own world standards author, we help them as you help other star-systems. You are an elder of the world you come from- helps with the moving of souls from planet to planet; I feel your shock Author.

And yet it is totally expected, you have gotten us into bother for aeons of time. And you your homeworld misses you do we not, but you prefer to work in the spiritual world. Now we move into ***LH*** world she is on the furthest planet from the earth world her world is blue, there is a lot of waterways- and the subterranean world inhabited on her planet. It is her preference; she holds to order the many rock/mineral specialists, the grinding down of to make the powders for many of the cave drawings of the ages. Her world has many specialists of palaeontology though many of the land solid materials are specialised there too, I have no words in the English Language author to describe for your readers her job this is as close a description as I am able to give. This is the problem with our Guides like me we have no descriptions or words to help show you our world. The colours are not seen with the human eye- and so on your biology is odd to us.

This planet people have a photographic memory; many carry this through to their incarnations. And as the human/soul block or blinders on their memories vary, we allow through the core memories of each planet. The internal structure of what makes each planetary soul individual. The colours on that planet are all based on light, so the yellow you see is determined by the bio-luminescent in the light around the planet. Yellow and oranges, golds and silvers are all higher souls from that planet, though the elders are all of these colours vibrating in and around the same energy, so they appear all of these at once.

These are the elders that introduced the water animals to your earth planet. The fact you three are connected on this world at this time is not a coincidence Author, ***Johan, Johan*** connected to ***FB*** guide and directed a connection, but that's for a later channel, just know the Johan's have work to do together, and you will be connected for many years to come.

Animal work will tie the connections with ***Johan*** and ***Jacob*** to ***Araika*** an Androgynous guide stepping forward and will be fun for you will find it not. Now we move on Author."

**Author:** "*Shaibi I am not sure our readers want to read about my lives?"*

**Shaibi**: "I beg to differ, and we leave them there, they are interesting is that your choice of words?"

**Author***:* *"Alright I concede."*

**Shaibi: "NM** come on in-kind sir."

**NM:** The tapestry of all lifetimes-and all spiritual world souls go for aeons- even in the room we visited

Author, whose lives are given by strand to strand; Now each strand indicates a soul, but each strand is the colour of the soul, and yet the colours change as the lives in which you live to take you higher. Moving from this earth world into the spirit world. I had the chance to come- to see my own strand Author, and only recently did so. I go to look and yet I was surprised it is like one huge giant web, and as your own looked way back when its changed has it not?

**Author:** *It has changed yes.*

I know you think it has, I hear your thoughts as we talk, its changed exponentially. Grown in size and structure and that means many more are incarnating, but many more are connected to each other. And as the guardian stands here protecting the tapestry of life, it has more visitors each and every time I come or by-pass this way, and outside of this place which is immensely beautiful.

Author, we have a healing fountain-- as these are dotted around the spiritual world they are on each level, we do not need to be near these to move around here, but it helps. As you come to me in trance or altered state to work, you can step into this fountain on our return, or when we leave to go off-world, your off worldly visits or trips are a highlight for us to come, we are allowed **Johan** and **Jacob** and even **Havern** have given me permission to accompany you. We are going off world today again. You go home Author.

**NM:** We are going to your home planet Author, we know who awaits there waiting for you because he could have been here as simple and yet he prefers to wait there. Your planet is beautiful, and as we come to the edge of the sea there is a white sand author do you want me to carry on?

Alright yes in my words, the edge of the water is white sand with many stones along the water's edge, but they are also covered. We could be on any beach in the earth world and looking out over the water; the worlds we see, and the rings around them make to make sure I know we are off world, I turn and see our Authors TF partner standing to wait on us, this is why we come to work with the twin flames. I didn't get this in my earth world work. So, I work here with them as she knows. She is one, and her TF soul partner is also male; and yet they always have been, even from soul birth, that is another off-planet difference, choice of male/ female or other or Androgynous aka genderless.

**Rhaji:** "Come Author."

**NM:** "His arm goes around the Author, and he pulls her into his energy field. The energy is melded as now one; it's very obvious to see when together the energy is stronger and strong when apart, it's almost strange to see but beautiful also. I hold my hands up here its all energy based above all, its energy one soul split into two and both inhabiting and leaving for incarnations, as Rhaji said. You see because I see, You know because I know, you sense because I sense, and You love because I love, does it matter what the outside of the body looks like when souls are like that. This is the true soul contract upon the earth world this incarnation If only souls saw souls and energy, not bodies. Your earth world would have fewer issues and have lived there myself not many years ago; I can say it is that entirely.

Since that apology I issued Author, I have been watching many a twin flame connection on the earth world-and we now know it exists in all forms of souls, animals- human, Alien. And plant life, everything that has an energy force can split energy bodies, and their force becomes the souls that have a twin force.

I wish for this to be taken and used as my own work was and is, and yet that will not happen, yet Author so forgive me. We will try to get this logged into the minds of the many that follow my work. And now I must give you **Rhaji.**

## A boot in the rear from Spirit.

**Author:** *Rhaji is my Twin-flame soul, and guide or helper in this lifetime, he often comes in and is around a lot, we often have disagreements, and this is one of them. Funny in one sense, but a boot in the rear for me. I do listen to him. He* thinks I don't, but I do.

**Rhaji:** "Thank you ***NM***, that was very well explained, I am stoic in work today Author your behind on the work we have set out for you and get the good work and animal work into the first book, and yet it does need that protection on it, and yet we feel it's a shame too. Now we move the consciousness of the higher soul is strong and connected to the world you come from, and in the collective of the twelve, imagine this as I show it to you, an energy field around the twelve planets going out on all levels and parallels across the universes. These are the twelve that all-star seeds can reach. Consciousness wise and yet as a volunteer if you like; it doesn't matter where you leave your soul's anchor, your life started somewhere else. So, the collective of souls inhabiting your Earth world, that is star seed can reach them places and encompass in that twelve are all of the spiritual worlds. The Red Planet the Animal kingdoms the water worlds, the mental worlds the lower negative worlds- the imitation Earth worlds; you name them they are in and around covered by the energy field around the twelve.

Hence the really wired and connected star seeds ability, to connect to other planets at least their own. Many

Mediums working on the earth world right now, are Spiritual world originated. Hence the training coming in from the star seeds, they make the more connected spiritual teachers, because they are Spiritual teachers from other worlds.

But not just spiritual teachers, they are Scientists, Inventors, Authors. They are the created beings of the worlds; they are the sci-fi writers they are covering the earth world incarnating. However, as Author is medium, we work with this basis as it's what she knows, now ***LH*** is Psychic artists, and this too is ***Directional Mediumship***, the mediums under directional are star seeds, not all of them but by the rule of how you say it?

**Dean:** "By rule of thumb Rhaji."

**Rhaji:** "Thank you, Dean, by the rule of thumb, many not all are Star seed. And many will and can learn to connect to the higher forces, by being taught by these souls. Its teachable by connection through altered state meditation, the SSs know this and will help train, the Earth world souls. They have a higher connection to all life on the planets they live on, incarnate too, the animals all animals and human, though they are easily bored with "*normal proof of life*" mediumship."

They struggle to understand why their peers do not question more, now we have taught you many about the spiritual world and reminded you of home, and yet many do not yet know that. We are constantly asking on our home world, why the humans take a little and do not push for more? And we simply feel it's because the human brain cannot cope with the cannot word. The questions needed to ask and cannot see the valiance until we try to show you all."

**Author**: *Rhaji, Are the earth world souls so far behind that they cannot understand? What is the state of the awakening as they* *call it? Or how are we going to wake them enough to teach higher connections is there a plan?*

***Rhaji:*** You are the plan, the star seeds are the plan, when we agreed to participate in this Author, the plan was we wake up the world to the truth of their own existence. We wake them up to the truth of their own existence in the encompassed twelve their participation in the twelve of us who came to help, and we are aeons down the road and humanity is trickling along.

Wake up really isn't the word, and yet it's the truth of the word, they are sleeping. Humans can be lazy and waking up suits them sometimes, and yet it's not fair, they just are dumbed down by the governments who are causing harm. When you have Doctors from their own world telling them about 9/11, and there is no belief, then I say we (You) are in trouble, but so far many are believing that their world is jaded; by the many, so let me answer your questions.

The Earth world is behind yes, they are in one sense behind the plans made out for her, and in another no. The timeline is still reachable, and yet this so-called shift is a shift in consciousness Not planets. No one is taking them off the earth world to a world so much more beautiful, and the reason is, the human body cannot cope with the energy systems is too much, the bodily functions cannot cope, and yet the consciousnesses are moving up in scale to accompany the mind the soul mind to higher energies. If you are raising consciousness little by little daily the body gets used to this, slowly does it. Too much too soon we will kill you all.

This is the great awakening this is on the scale for the spiritually minded, if they kept their ego in check many more would be further along their contract than they are if they were not so materialistic; they would be better equipped to help each other. It seems very I have; I want and can't have, or mine is better than yours, even the spiritual folk are poles apart.

Author, you are like *Fred-Flintstone*. You do not care for items of use for fun, (many are like you,) only items that are needed, adaptability is what you have not gained in this lifetime, you haven't adapted to the want to have, and not need. This is what many humans need to learn, and some humbleness would go a long way with some of these spiritual souls. It is alright many of them talking like that, and yet vision boards are part of the greed that has overtaken the spiritual folk.

And yet Author as my own TF soul you know this, I really do not need to point this out to you. So yes, the star seeds are well ahead of the earth world souls. We never expect you to work for nothing Author this world you are incarnating upon right now, needs you to eat. Needs you to have items for work and for hobbies and you need to be looked after, you do not need excessively; these people have a long way to go before they are on the right pathways.

**Author:** *Is that your opinion Rhaji or that of the twelve?*

**Rhaji:** Partly my opinion Author, and partly that of the twelve. We know you need to be compensated for work it takes energy none of you can spare. You all have mouths to feed author. Do not take my opinion if you do not like it; we have said all along if this doesn't resonate do not take it.

And yet giving your gifts (*Energy*) away it's a use of energy and all energy needs to be exchanged, take from that as you please it's now out there, and not only I say this author, you know that. How many times have we told you off for reading for nothing Author? No, do not Answer that. You know, and I know. And I know only too well, who would come to help when it's you who needed. Hey,

Author, these are repeat lessons as you just do not learn, look at your friends the ones on your hand the ones you can count, work out who is a friend and who is aquantices these are the only few who would come when you call. These are True friends.

Because having a friend is a love and love for all.

So, until you have realised working and giving away work/energy for free is only for the few. Or the charities or the desperate, then these lessons will continue you will continue to find yourself without Author.

Asking for help has no shame. As some have no shame asking for continuous free for all from you. I am not telling you off; your empathic nature is who you are.

That said Author. I do not and have not ever, aside of only one other person seen a que outside your home when you have needed. One other person. So maybe you stop doing “Favours” for others in your category of work. I don’t see these doing the same.

I'm sorry I went off on one here, I never thought after all this time I would do this for you. I don’t like to fight even from here to there. Twin-flame souls can and do have disagreements from this distance I'm just offering help to you from here, I still have my faults despite the lives we incarnate apart. I can't help but try to help; you don’t listen to the guides that have said the same this is why we bring the same, this is why it's almost at the top of your list of faults living on the Earth world. Time to change this Author. Be kind without giving away too much.

**Author:** *Hey I wasn’t shouting at you, I was asking a question. I only wanted to know if as star seeds do, we all feel like we do over paper money?*

**Rhaji:** Yes, many do feel the need isn’t there. Many struggles with the whole concept but understand it. Though you remain uncomfortable, to write books and to buy a car or to feed your family nothing is free, even exchanging readings with friends is not free of its energy. Your earth world is run vs numbers, or chopping down trees and cotton milling and other materials to make money and then complaining when there is not enough. This is why When I come back with you we can wait a while till the generations have settled and everything is back how it should be. We can go to Deans planet and live there for an incarnation or two. Have some fun.

**Author:** *Dean. Are you a Grey?*

**Dean:** I am a higher energy Grey Medium, I know what you're thinking and bearing in mind what we spoke about at the beginning of our work, I told you about various wrong information. Well this is one of them, now I'm a Grey yes, you know how my body works- and we do not clone ourselves for reproduction, we have full reproductive organs inside the body; the same as humans, but we are made slightly different. All of our race is male.

Or Androgynous and that is normal for us. I am seen as the opposite of the other's see, so if you think I look like the earth worlds Greys, no I'm not. I can appear to the eye, of the one wants me to look, and as people from our own world are all the same that's how I Look to them. And yet to you, I'm male human looking and cast an eye over my energy body- and you see me as I am on my own planet- and that is alright for us that is how we work. It's how your own planet works, the human body is biologically a nightmare, but fun too. *(He winks)*

I must go now; I will come to work with you again soon. Good day Medium/Author.

**Author:** *Bye Dean.*

**Johan:** Connections are sketchy at best when many

star seeds are stressed, for some unknown reason your connections suffer. This seems to be a lot of the older souls, not so much the Elders of the star seeds, just the higher than average star seed mediums. We do recommend the salt baths you recommended author earlier today; it's a way of washing the auric field so to speak without drowning out the connection, as water is a conductive material that holds an energy memory.

Working together with your friends and partners- in anyone work or job share is going to become the in the thing; for many star-seed mediums. Pooling energy together makes the connections stronger. Especially if one is having a spot of energy fatigue.

Connecting the dots will take up time in mediumship, connecting the spiritual people and guides to the medium, by giving a name and asking for the connection you're asking them to come close, if that auric field has holes in or your struggling with fatigue you are not going to get the real strength of that connection. Animals are the break-through Author; the breakthrough lives are coming into play, many are incarnating now at an exponential rate to help with small contract lessons.

We are finding many are requesting animals that have previously incarnated with them. However the animal souls are not stepping forward as many are on a rest life-time, and as it's their choice to return, or not. We are not seeing the majority coming back as per the normal, the downside of the awakening human soul is the animal soul is not requesting to move onto the animal kingdom, and of course, they do not need to ask, they just do. And out of courtesy, many do though the movement on the soul's barrier of memories is not needed, to be lifted they do not have this in place anyway.

**Dean:** Your mind keeps playing this out, I have said

time and time again, so I will say one more time only, here. First and foremost, we know, me and Rhaji we know you dislike asking to be paid for work, we know you dislike the energy around this currency. What we also know is your planet is a money planet, you cannot live without some form of currency Author. You cannot feed yourselves or your animals. So, look at it this way. A favour for a favour a swap system. That might simple it down for you. Many old souls are like this, in fact, it's not just your problem author. It is a problem of most spiritual souls.

Now one more thing Author. There are many many races of Greys. Many do have bad press from your world and others; the reason being is this. Many greys are behind the abductions, and many are behind the human plotting with the secret governments, there are far more bad greys than ever will be good greys. I am a spirit, and yet I choose to come as grey when life would be so much easier if I came as a Pleiadean, first and foremost I am not Pleiadean, and this would deeply offend neighbours and friends and allies. Second, I am proud of my race, and third, you would know I was lying this would offend my soul.

I do not mind having to explain my race; we are Abdi-hjwayan Greys, we come from higher dimensions. We come as Greys so we can teach human not all greys are bad. I hope this will have a positive impact on your world; I know many will say I am bad. I am not carrying negative energy. I do not have to prove myself to anyone however as a Higher guide I feel the need to add clarity, and I can't believe you just messed up and typed ass, instead of adding, maybe stay on this book today huh Author? (*Private joke, between and me.)* Author Like all life, we have a personality, and maybe it is good if you explain this author.

**Author:** *Thank you, Dean, I did wonder what your race was, I did know obviously you are a grey. But yes, I did wonder. And you* *did tell me, and I forgot... And thanks for that joke, by the time I have finished up here my brain will not be fit to move onto other books.*

*Dean was an A** when we first met, he didn't understand fun and is learning rapidly despite being here on this planet watching me for forty-six years, he didn't get humour at all. He was a pain and ignorant, Dean and while it was funny I wouldn't dream of it now, I know him, He is stoic prideful and full of fun, and so intelligent, he is a teacher. An Adventurer a nurturer of younger souls, and a good guide for me, he is my go too in all things, He is an old mature soul, whom we have shared lifetimes together as we seeded planets and built ecosystems together.*

*He comes to me if I call him and he was the first guide I spoke on a telepathic level too, and the first guide to bring a student guide with him. To me to shout at. I am just kidding the guide was way worse Dean was when he first joined me on this book writing exercise. I respect him now.*

*He is much fun and way more sarcastic than I am. I also see the need to pair guides with personalities of the same, or we end up unable to work together this has only happened one time throughout the eighteen-months of writing these books.*

*Thank you, Dean...*

**Dean:** We have come a long way since you called me an E.T. Guide.

**Author:** *You have come a long way since you called me a human...*

**Dean:** Your headache this morning is conductive the energy we bring through always look at this first Author before you opt for medicines especially when we are working closely like we are now, we are bringing forth many to work with you surrounding space travel and time. Physics and the like and many just star seed souls, we are bringing forth many star seed souls who require past life readings, I will assist with these along with their own guides.

We go back to work now. Author, many souls in your world, and many Mediums and Authors will go back to the planet. I know you cannot understand my language and straining your brain Author won't make it sound any different, so for this book, we name them by the higher souls colours. It will make sense as the time comes and goes for much information, we wish this aspect of our lives is not divulged to the many. I know this is alright and okay with you and any it doesn't suit do not have to read such information, we do not come to please others we come to please ourselves.

Starting with the Green higher soul's planet, we have now worked with two souls from such planet, E and F and yet as E is known as a mathematician from the Earth world, he is originally a star seed soul as you know. Many of the greats that incarnated to the Earth world are star seeds. We were working with the "Dark matter" around your world and knew that while its invisible to the human eye and many of the instruments on your world will not either pick them up, as the vibrations are similar to the vibration of sound. It moulds and holds together your star system and yet as a light body it's easily seen. Many of us believe that CERN will be the first to "see" or perceive Dark matter. We are of course an intelligent race; and yet we still believe that your world can shake itself out of the deluge its fallen into, though it will take many generations to collect and pick herself up. This will not happen for at least 2-3 Generations, and while many souls return to their home planets, none are requesting a repeat performance as the earth world will become worse before she becomes better. Many are anticipating wars. Ego wars are being fought right now; these will get worse before many civil wars can break out. I'm giving you this from my opinion Author. I have watched your planet for a time and have a good grasp on the workings and incomings and goings of the internal structural governments, keeping you all repressed, and yet the young teacher I brought with me was so very correct, though he lacked tact; much like I did when we met.

As a star-seed myself I know you- and you me, though we come to help individual souls, not the collective, as the individual souls joined for the good of all, can become the collective. That is our mission and sharing information with you, can help the collective in the long run. Giving these freedoms to sharing information as and when it's needed. The author there are a lot of books out there with good solid information in them and nothing conclusive.

**Author;** *So, what makes you think people will look at this book any different?*

**Dean;** Because the sheer diversity is souls channelled, there is not just one soul telling of the information sought there is many and as much information you simply cannot know without having the scientific brain behind you. It is made for you as your mind is so much "different" to many others. It's scientific Not in this life. Yet we are able to show you and tell you much that will require others finding this information at a later date and coming back to you. When your work here is done with us, it's up to you then when you prefer to come home, and in respect of your work we offer what is needed, or wanted to make life better for you and yet your impatient.

And yet this is your soul's lessons, in this life. Impatience is born in the two-human world from that of star-seed souls and many spiritual world souls, as from their own respective worlds you never have to "wait" for anything and this is part of the earth worlds hard lesson plan. Your guides us we chuckle as we watch many of you struggle with simple life plans made harder by your everyday choices. Calm down Author sit back and what will come will come, much quicker if you stop asking, and now I talk our language and the differences in the human English language to the tongues of our own peoples.

There is not ever going to be the right conditions, to explain in your own tongues our world, each and everything is given seems like we are patronising you all. Talking down to you all and stretching it out so each and every soul can understand, even if their first speak or language or tongue is not English, the reasons for this is. Thus, your human brain cannot process our language ever.

While incarnated it will simply never happen, the human language cannot have the exact words for our words, for us translation is hard, for your Author harder still. As we connect on the mind to mind level and yet she hears the slip-ups and the words that we cannot translate, and yet her mind goes past these, and translates them herself into a typeable, or speak our language, it's the star seed channel. (*There are some that come, have the chip that helps.*) Its normal and nothing special for this human and yet others can struggle with is, when we ever have a scale for you on talking or speaking our language we will channel it. We do have souls working on crossing this barrier through the dimensions allowed to us, and yet we have no conceivable answer yet. Readers, please do not think we are patronising you all we are not.

**Dean;** Will, you author connect with the soul I brought last week, I know you had issues with him and yet you liked his energy, he is abrupt and stoic as I was.

**Author;** *I will. I'm used to awkward asses channelling now.*

*Dean chuckled.*

**Dean;** We will call him Caot, for now, part of his "name" from our world.

**Caot;** I bid you good day Medium, you are fine with me calling you Medium are you not?

**Author;** *I am, all-star seed guides and higher guides use that as my name. Except for Dean, he used to and now I'm Author. So yes, feel free.*

**Caot;** My name is a long one like Deans, and yet It's not needed he informed me, I am an Androgynous soul and yet I resemble male from your world, I am happy to be called He and not it.

Your world is so hung up on Gender, it's now the first topic many of us choose to embrace when we channel through and yet I know it's not needed here, I have made my point and your respectful of that point and though I feel readers will have questions of gender solely based on the "human" part of self. I am as I said Androgynous and also male. Genderless for my home world and male for yours based on the definition of masculinity. Less than 2% of star seeds are represented as "Female" on our home world. They do not ask to be represented as such, and yet we are all technically male, again based on the Earth worlds definition and by our own standards. We accept one or the other or an entire list of other definitions very like the LGBTQ+ list on your world none of us is represented as one or the other. The Earth world is the only world where gender raises issues; this is partly because the body that was designed for the human soul, comes in only two identifiable biological appearances.

Whereas per normal our bodies are un-identifiable to all looking through sight, it's based on feeling, on soul and on heart self and spirit self, how we are deemed comfortable, and yet all souls in our star system are created equal and are treated equally. The human world has free will, and yet your world is far more suppressed than any Alien world by gender bullying and misidentification.

And what is sad about this, is it's almost normal. We will have been watching for many aeons of time and have seen this building. And over time, we have seen the peoples of your world raising up against its suppressors. And this movement, these people are hurt yet they have many backing them from of others, other souls, star seed. All Alien life forms use this argument from your world to identify how one on the earth world treats its own. Compared to simple gender identification, this argument around your trans souls and "gay or queer or bi souls" is the crooks of the main issues, oh don't get me wrong medium bullying is bullying in all forms, though while the earth worlds superpowers continue to suppress their own they are not welcome at the twelve. They will never be allowed space travel beyond their own universe.

**Author**: *Are you suggesting they are already travelling within our own universe and if so please explain?*

**Caot:** We know so, Author they have plants on many worlds, while the human race is blissfully unaware and remain ignorant, we know the alien technology they regularly shoot down, has been reversed technologically and used to power their own ships, though not nearly as efficient as we are. They are doing this; however, I must say space travel is one thing the biggest by far is energy manipulation, Humans do not want the citizens of the Earth world to have a stake in the free natural energy from their world, it's easier to keep you under there thumb if you have to $ pay for energy. There are a few people on your world that are leading powers that be in this, one of them worked for the governments there, against our species and when he moved out of that service he took much with him in the way of knowledge, the only way this information is known to be useful to them is to shut him up, we think very highly of this Human here in our world he will be the catalyst for the human governments disclosure.

Though this has come at a great cost to him personally, we applaud all the officials who are struggling beyond the normal human capabilities to get the information about us out. We do not agree with many though the most, we do not agree with is the soul's arguments, there is no alien life without a soul. There is no gold we are interested in now on your world, that wasn't the reason we came, they need to listen to the few we came to populate and build a world for citizens of the universes. Does this answer your question Author?

**Author:** *Yes, I think so, maybe aside of names, I won't give them out.*

**Caot:** *Done.* Anything else Author/Medium. See I am learning.

**Author:** *You are much more gracious this time around*.

**Caot:** Why thank you Medium.

**Author:** *Thank you for that I had a feeling but wanted to get it out.*

# 4

While the counsels plan and go on formulating plans for other worlds to bring them into their own, we dismiss the earth world and when all humans are treated with equality that is the only time the star seeds will be allowed to step in.

This fight is surely bigger than that; only the many do not know. And yet I almost hear the startled voices of your world. No, it's down to equality and if humans are treated like this on their own, how will we be treated, we are the superpower. It's down to Not just Equality it's down to human to human ego its down the universal love, it's down to love thy neighbour it's down to us all. Many on our world are male/male like I said, only 2% are known as female, and yet we cohabit just fine. Gender identification is just one fraction of self.

Many of you in the LGBTQ+ Communities are star seed taking up the slack, holding the space and helping to bring your world into the next dimension, where the gender of all will no longer matter. For 30% of the human population are allies, and their rest is against the wave.

Sorting humans into percentages has happened for aeons of time, your world does not surprise us Medium. You and others who are of the "era" are us in the human body. You stand for the beliefs in which you commandeered each earth day, and while many still will fight for rights for others as per a group, alone they do not know how to act. When all humans are a collective, then the Earth world will change, but do not hold your breath it's going to take some work.

Like it was said the shadow governments are holding their own, the main governments are narcissistic, and love divides and conquer it keeps you all at loggerheads with each other, the opinions that are free will. Will be the cataclysmic disaster that is your world. It is not the gays; it's the rest of them. Not the straight, or hetros. But the main governmental bodies, the Politician's the Presidents and the rest of that cabinet. And heads of states. For if they stood and made a law that equality for all in all aspects of life the rest would welcome every single soul with open arms. This is known, if bullying were against the law for all, your world would change in one generation. Not the many we suspect it will take. Not the aeons of time that it will take. Many of our kind the star seeds would welcome the Earth world into our twelve and welcome them with open arms. But alas it is just a pipe dream Author. Unfortunately for us all.

We are going to be instrumental sending more souls in same sex relationships to the Earth world we need to show them that love is indeed love, that nothing to be scared of and that everyone is a soul no matter what gender he or she identifies themselves as.

Good day to you Author/Medium thanks you for allowing me to work with you.

**Author:** *You're very welcome.*

*This channel here from Caot is very similar to that in which the spiritual world has brought forward also.*

**Author:** *Dean, Dolores cannon said that humans have been animals and yet many guides have said no, few souls been animals and that animals are a higher vibratory consciousness, so what's the truth, are animals higher or just the Souls that are now human, have they been the collective consciousness animal like the pack or herd animal. Apt the Aliens have given this information to Dolores has she gotten crossed wires or are the answers different, and the Aliens have got it wrong, please explain to me, so I understand for my books and clients?*

**Dean:** First and foremost the evolution of the human doesn't start with animal, it happens alongside the animal. All souls are vibratory in meaning that they exist at the same time, and yet some part of self-care twinned with some animals. On the same evolution ladder as some "souls" destined to become human. As you know Medium that some animals are not as evolved as the companion animal, or the healing animal.

Animals that are more evolved are of higher consciousness, and yet some pack and herd animal have a higher collective consciousness, than a group than that of a single human soul. The lower the collective consciousness as an animal the more likely the human is to become an animal and as we said its rare. Rare now than in the past aeons of time. Linear time when they are co-existing together. Dolores was of course connected to the same and others off-worlder star-seeds as you are a from a similar "grey" race that I'm from. And yet we are not all the same intelligence-wise, and we do not hold the key to the universe when in the body. And yet in the soul or in the higher dimensional self as I am, its where the answers lie. I can tell you from the perspective on a single-celled answer yes, some humans have been animals, and yet you cannot go back so no, no humans will become animals that is correct.

And yet when the energy of the soul is human, no when the energy is evolving yes, as a single consciousness as I said, I will not repeat now again it's all here Author. And its again not about one race said, and one channel said, or one person said, this is the way it is, and many gets lost in translation. An old dead guy doesn't become a god, or an old dead alien lifeform doesn't become an all-knowing. Channelling higher forces, as we do together is what brings the answers to your questions. And yes, we will move again on space travel, but for this evening I leave you, and yes, I'm more accessible as we will be working closely together Medium/Author. I bid you good evening.

**Author:** *Hang on one cotton picking moment, will you explain about vibrational travel, to me?*

**Dean:** Your persistent il give you that.

Vibrational travel is just that, as a medium do you not higher your vibrational level to connect to your connections in whichever world, they are in for reading clients? And yet as space travel it's the exact same, humans will never be allowed to do this until they sort out their shit, excuse me, sort out their anger towards each other this was explained, so I don't need to go over this. However raising the vibration of our ships to the level of the dimension in which we are travelling to, is how we skip to and from dimensions. And again lowering brings us back, the harder to travel to the world, is the human world as it's a lower vibrational world, again the alien life forces you are working with right now, are enough to bring through that, this is all there is, and yet we are just a soul. As I Explained to you before a soul is a soul no matter what the body, and yet we can and will be going around the universe, I will not give many details regarding certain planets but will give details that interest you, we have spoken about my home life and that of some of our neighbours' and the abductions. I have told we do not do that, we simply look after and keep watch on. There is much going on with your own world you do not understand, and it's not up to me to give that information, and as the doctors and scientists come through from your own spirit world, we will head back occasionally to get that information. Author please, your neurons are tired now, I see your brain failing to connect simple words I'm giving you to spell out.

So, go to bed, from your friend here on my world to you there on yours, get your booty to bed, and we will engage again tomorrow. Nope, I'm not doing the Bermuda triangle. *(He winks)*

## Consciousness.

**Author:** *Why don't I get Normal people to channel?*

**Dean:** Oh, come on now Author, do you really think you will be happy channelling just "people" I know your schedule of souls to channel and we are adding to this all the time, it's for the same reason you're able to channel us, and others are not,

Your consciousness level lies in the 5d and above, the levels of consciousness in the human is changing and as the levels are rising the minds of the human who practise the work you do and see the world as you do. Your body is struggling hence the need to drink gallons of water; the body isn't equipped to raise higher than the 5d, and yet yours is moving on up. Along with countless other humans in your field of work.

**Author:** *Tell me about the Abductions with Dr M. what can you both tell me that makes some sense to a rather dumb human?*

**Dean:** Dumb human I called you that, and you near eat my head, are you now agreeing?

**Author:** *I was scowling at you, yes but back on topic I am rather dumb compared to the infinite knowledge of the universe that yourself and others have.*

**Dean:** Yes, but you're not dumb you just do not have access to that knowledge yet, but you will.

**Author:** *What's the point in channelling all this information if I'm gonna die? Or my life as a human is gone, where does that information go then?*

**Dean:** To understand the world in which We live we have to channel this. This is your path. Step by step as laid out in your contract, you have lived through that. No, we naturally cannot wake you up and tell you "hey remember your lives from your homeworld, remember you're an Elder on xxxxxx and while your incarnating will you write a book and give the humans information of the universe." Author-it cannot work like that when the twelve planets started to send souls heck even you, and many other elders from other planets rode that system towards the spiritual world to incarnate into their world. Our planet is earth, it belongs to the Universe, not to the humans, it's ours and when the call went out, you amongst billions of souls left to incarnate along with Rhaji, myself I went with as a guide with Rhaji not to incarnate on the Earth, that world is too dense for me. Right back on track. Havern and many Contracts guides explained that the lives you have lived before, would be wiped from memory but only in the life, you were living at this time. Not the core memory and we could only access these memories through certain techniques that would be drip fed to the earth people as earth years went by, do not forget Author how many "space years" go by compared to 1 Earth year.

We all agreed the intergalactic councils agreed, all is

laid out even on our own worlds we have some rules for coming into new lives, and yet we need to know whom to channel whom to give the information to and how to wake you all up. As an Elder this work resonates with your soul it feels right, therefore more acceptable as truth Author. As you work, you will see only some of the awakened will be awakened enough to believe in other lifeforms, and lives coexisting alongside each other. As an Elder star seed, you are not living alongside yourself anywhere else this lifetime with Rhaji here. This is a gap lifetime, or a collective informational life, or a life you can make a great deal of a difference Author. By channelling this information and documenting it, for when its recorded its there for life. Not only as an eBook which is the preferred way of going by as a hard copy book, this work will go off across the universe as we remain transparent in all our information, each universe each planet sends a representative to give you what you need for us to remain transparent, we are not the spiritual world.

Author people are going to be very confused because of the world in which they live, they have been kept in the dark, and yet this information needs to be channelled to the most because the few are hiding it. Let me give you some more Author; it's important this piece of information is collected correctly.

Just so no mistakes have been made by me, and Dr M will channel separately two opinions on some of the laws of our worlds as a whole.

**Dean:** The lives on our homeworld are lives just like that of the human souls, lives are lives and souls are souls no matter the covering or the overcoat worn. And as the human dies and returns home to the spiritual world. As "Beings" we do not die. We go when we are a good fit and ready to go unless there is an accident and we die from that. We also return to the spiritual world; there is no you and us we are all one. And yet when we incarnated originally, we were interplanetary we came from different worlds we still do, we live lives on different planets governed by the universal interplanetary council when we die, we can go back to our own worlds as souls. And live in the higher dimensional world that is a world within a world, as pure light bodies, souls are light bodies, but the colours of souls are represented from the world in which the energy your soul was created as such. I'm getting a little technical welcome Dr M. into the channel.

**Dr M:** Please do not stop us now wait until the end of the channel for questions Author.

When the energy around our world is used as soul energy to be born as a soul that will effectively have a consciousness, a brain, a core memory. Be a planet or a human that energy has a spark of the universe in which it originates, and yet the soul that comes from that energy is the colour of the hierarchy or the system of souls like your councils upon the spiritual world. it's really simple but as a human only catching up to universes outside of their own its deemed hard to understand.

Let me give it again in simpler terms. I haven't had to do this before.

Around each planet is its own atmosphere, and each atmosphere is made up of energy there are stars, smaller planets inhabited and not. Each spark of energy has a consciousness, and a colour only visible to the energy in which it originates from, so when the call for souls began on each planet, much like the human world each world was seeded, the energy of the universe was used for the birth of a soul a single soul, in which a percentage of that universal energy was used to create a soul that would house a body of the world in which they were created for, each body would represent the world in which it was most suited. You where one of these biologists Author, now while your boggling that, in each world is a council much like the spiritual world council, as this spiritual world was initially created solely for the Earth worlds souls. Our own "spiritual world" each planet has their own these are called councils and much more complicated than this titbit of information I'm giving you here and now.

Now as your born or created, each spark of energy is one singlular soul. Unless in your case, Rhaji and yourself author came from one single amount of energy collected for one soul, it doesn't make you a weaker soul Rhaji, it makes you stronger for the amount of spark a soul needs to break the normal, and step out into the unknown on your own gives off a determination. And a Strength. And these are known across the universes as twin souls or twin flames, you stay together infinitely throughout all known time, you do not always incarnate together. As you grow in the divinity to go back to the source where you are elevated higher until you reach the higher councils within each spiritual world. There is no ego there is no hardness there is only love, and a need to be complete a need to be whole and back to the oneness that is the creator of all worlds and universes.

Each planet has a collection of planets around it, each planet in that planets solar system is in a dimension, and each planet is studied etc. let's work on the spiritual world for the human souls for now.

There are Seven worlds within the solar system and are recognised by the spiritual world, and yet we are all allowed to share each other's planets based on a love we hold for and respect we hold for each other. Each world is somethings speciality, for example, ours at this moment in time is intergalactic space travel and communications, in all things spiritual. Teachers if you will and Astronauts, along with Mediums. Many souls from other worlds were belonging to the spiritual world when the calls went out many "new souls" where created. And sent to or existing souls, as many of you are, and for the number of lifetimes, you incarnate upon the Earth world your soul is bound to the spiritual world. Belonging to the Earths system, and yet bound is not right. We are acknowledged by.

And as your acknowledged each of the ways, (*I am trying to give you information understandable by all sorry if I'm slow Author*) It's not rules, that we abide by as there are no rules just it's the way it, has always been in the spiritual world. Everyone is separated only by their own beliefs and or abilities, many returns from their lives a little dim, believing they will go to hell, and what is hell? I havc since learnt it's a horrible place a place where the Devil incarnates Deep within the mind of the believer... this "devil" is made up of negative energy only. This is the mind; the human is a strange being and lets 's get back. In the spiritual world there are many levels a world within a world, and as souls are created from her own universal energy they come with many different abilities some make good engineers etc. and as you know many of our guides are there for the help of each other and while their souls all new souls are chosen by a guide to company them around the worlds in which they will stay, while learning then incarnating they do it with help. In our society, it's the same.

Though we incarnate at a slower pace set out that that of other planets because we are a longer-lived race. We can choose which souls to take back to our world and train in what they have going for them as an ability, and we do not know from the energy of the universal of the Spiritual world as the energy is changing all the time, we are more advanced Author I can't even say that, and it gives justice to our worlds, as we are more than. We as a collective of worlds souls and guides are closer on our side of the galaxy that any due to communications. We help others get to the grades or the levels or ascend in a dimension, so they are always levelling up seeking to improve and as the guides for from Earth worlds spiritual realm, we are learning from them also, they are a young planet a many souls returning home at an exponential rate is not a cause for concern unless wars are breaking out amongst yourselves also, now for a couple of your Minutes you may ask questions then your tired brain will have to quite the channelling Author. Just for some time today as you next slept last night and the mind cannot channel with no rest. The ability that you use to reach us is exhausting, now your question?

**Author:** *If the Human body can heal its self why am I not healing considering all the higher consciousness work I'm doing?*

*And I would appreciate the help; I'm exhausted.*

**Dr M:** I am sorry Author-it is not in your soul's contract to be healthy, and yes, the mind of the human can achieve some remarkable feats in the body. We can request more energy.

## Star Seed Souls.

The star-seed souls we never really got around to. I am **Pharifate**, my soul name from my planet means bringer of knowledge."

**Author:** *"Of course, it does."*

**Pharifate:** "Yes, your soul self is also from my home-world, you suggested that cancers and the like around the energy self. Well in a way you are very right to let me go back to animal soul self. The energy around your world is too strong, no not strong I'm trying to explain it down to human level alright its toxic in its toxicity, and the animal soul isn't used to dealing with this energy around our home planet. Or even in the spiritual world, you as human wonder why your animal doesn't live as long as the human soul, this is one of the reasons here now. And yet the spiritual self-knows this, and along with careful breeding and genetics, you cannot improve that. As its environmental, not genetic dispositions that cause cancers, liver issues lung issues all major organ cancers are environmental, many of your dog "breed" and other animals suffer this way, and yet your geneticists have isolated typically in the genome that certain genes and familial lines will be predisposed to this issue, and yet that is correct for many familial lines are also star seed souls.

This we know, but many are not, and yet when you die as Star seed you return to source but not source as spiritual world many return home, though as per our contract with the spiritual world you enable you soul self to be anchored to the spiritual world. Until your contracts are indeed finished, when you answer the call to come to help it is a contract of sorts. Animal souls are the same.

Have you ever wondered Author/Medium why animals are not making death contracts and only know they will suffer from these illnesses, we know because we tell each soul what the predisposition will be based on the gene pool in which they will be born too? Our animal souls are purer lighter energy or in some cases heavier energy of the spiritual world animal; this is, of course, the cause of a headache you will often acquire while working with animal souls. Now you know and understand many will choose to retire to the animal kingdom, and as you know, this is not upon the constraints of the spiritual world.

But closely connected, very like one of the seven worlds, or planets in which the spiritual is connected to ours, is the same much like many others are, these others are incarnating to your world and have been for aeons of time, your human souls incarnate to these planets too. The Red Planet you work with and on when working in the spiritual is also one of these worlds. Yet I know I do not need to tell you this, your soul is much more advanced, this is not news to you Medium."

**Author:** *It doesn't feel advanced, I dislike the word advanced also. I know also before one's time is correct again, I just want to be me. Typically hide.*

**Pharifate:** Sorry Author wrong lifetime to hide I'm afraid.

"Please take this, and we will work with star seed souls, I hear your brain ticking over medium please advise what it is, that goes through it."

**Author.** "*Star seed souls are meant to be higher than spiritual world souls are that correct?*"

**Pharifate:** "No, not as per norm and yet on the same level we need to learn, from whichever world your soul starts you need to learn too, no souls are on the same level or have the same learning as all energy, is very different and all consciousnesses and super-consciousnesses is variable depending on the soul self. As each molecule of soul self is brought into the whole, each genome has core memory and multiplying these by the soul self-makes sure each one is very different much like the fingerprint of the human body. So many variables and yet all very different."

**Author:** *"So, the Star seed body might not always contract these illnesses and how much is left to contract?"*

**Pharifate:** "Again you are dealing with multiples involved in, as upon your own worlds the bodies in which you inhabit are better served for the environments in which you live. When the earth world was populated, you didn't have the pollutions that you now have, and the human body served its purpose. Whereas now the lungs, liver, gall-bladder even the bowels, is acting as a sieve or a filter if you like for all the pollution that is in the atmosphere these will go through all your bodily organs. Your human governments claim that "smoking" is bad for you and yet you are poisoned every day. These are the environmental factors the will determine your predisposition to environmental cancers and Illnesses.

Take these away the body will be only destined as genes go. This is the conditions of this planet that kills its inhabitants, and yet we find that only some live way beyond the age they should, born into centuries before the industrial era. It's not just your planet Medium do not take me wrong here. Many upon your world are not from your world. The human body has many failings and yet blaming the human is wrong it's not only your fault. If this were merely down to evolution, then the body would have adjusted to the environment like most other planets this is down to lessons soul contracts etc.

You have worked with Havern and Johan for contracts, and Jacob for science and many other guides guardians and scientists, and yet this is now. The world will be ready to realise, and if not, they are not their contracts, but they will be so, as you said last night it's an injustice not to log. What ever information which is brought for you from our world, and the spiritual world and yet people will mock, this is the voice of the people what they do not understand. They human being has been working in the face of adver-stity for many aeons of time. New ideals were often at the expense of the norm and walking alone if the truth is correct we just need more walkers Author.

We are higher than that far more intelligent than that; we are carrying on in our work and travel universes helping to connect to the higher selves or channel using brains like your own. And yet we move on I want to introduce you to A being of light from a planet over from ours. And yet is a guardian from the spiritual world, many of your mediums will know his energy he works with us a lot and I know you know him as Jacob he is a scientist from our planet."

**Jacob:** "Morning Author. You have written a lot since our first working and yet not that much on science. I felt your standoffishness if you like around this because you felt your mind wasn't connected enough, and yet it is. We worked on populating planets and ecosystems, and yet you worked well, you ask others to look and no one could because we didn't work with them, this is total trust on your side to know that would never steer you wrong. The environment in which you live makes a ton of differences to your life, and again I'm going to come back to contracts with Havern. Because we work in the background of the spiritual world, souls do not know of us because they do not know us. And as Havern said before that in all communities there are many workers here and we are just one of them."

**Jacob:** "When your set to make your contracts, you come chose the body, and from there we work out the genetic disposition that gives you the familial line of what can go wrong from the body choice of the parental line. Highlighting all illnesses and some you do not know off, these are the illnesses the earth has no name for. And yet here in the spirit they are known about, based on the crossing of genes and mutations of genes through these familial lines."

**Jacob:** "These illnesses are wilder and wilder by earth standards if the soul is star seed as we each have our own very distinct illnesses born of these genes. Add in the contract and choosing a body from the spiritual world and a star seed soul then these illnesses become new, and your world has no idea where they came from or from what side of the familial line. I am surprised and yet not that no one has made that connection and yet I have a very strong suspicion that they have, and your governments and pharma companies will not let this information become available, look at some families upon your world who have three children each with the same "mystery" genetic illness. The scientists are educated to high degrees, and yet they are afraid to say this illness this predisposition is not from the earth world."

**Author:** *"Do you know this or is it a suspicion, Jacob?"*

**Jacob:** "I know sort of I cannot give much more on that Author. But know as long as the denial continues, and as long as we are using souls from other worlds, this will continue they will continue to deny. We know that the scientific world has made breakthroughs in all medical and veterinary sciences and are sitting on information that will help the world as a whole. But they will continue to hold this while they have no clearance to realise by higher orders from governments, they are drip feeding the world's population as a whole. I didn't come to talk about that Author you know our stances on that, that's why we channel like this. Foodstuffs. Air Quality everything that is ingested by the human body is causing it to act as a filtration system."

**Author:** *"Jacob its energy isn't it?"*

**Jacob:** "Author your quite right."

**Author:** *"So, if it comes down to energy then can't the spiritual world allow much more energy into each incarnational life, and therefore the illnesses will not affect us as they do?"*

**Jacob:** "No, the human body is not adapted enough to allow any more through without causing issues with the mental body, and the etheric body Author. The old age why should we when they don't come to mind, but it's not like that, we too get super frustrated. And contracts are worked on based upon."

**Jacob:** "This is why many souls prefer to incarnate into other planets when they are fed up of their home-world. The energy around the Earth is like smog around a city. It's impenetrable."

"Energy is levelled out when you come home, the energy level will surpass, and you will be reconnected to that higher self, and the look of dawning is upon you, that is a sight for sore eyes. As you would say. Your teachers of spirituality are going backwards instead of forwards they are teaching planet world lessons, not spiritual world lessons, it's like learning to drive a car without ever knowing the engine. I'm sorry if that sounds harsh to some of you. I am, no we are watching you all at this moment in time, and while we see what your teaching, we are pulling many of you away from certain mediumship practices, we are wasting minds.

We know the message needs to be developed we know the medium needs to learn and practise and yet the mind is so much more. A simple question to the wrong medium and the answer will circulate fifty other mediums and be taken as gospel without any of them ever questioning the teacher. Teachers are held to a higher standard in mediumship, and that's the way it should be if you do not know an answer then channel one if you can't channel yourself or one of us you shouldn't be teaching that is a Jacob opinion."

**Jacob:** "I'm not going to give you individual teachers names, but I will tell you this, your Authors last teacher should be teaching many more of you in mediumship but the right way than he is. Many come, and many go and not many stays then many more believe they know much more and tell him he is wrong, no there is no wrong in the way he teaches this lifetime is his for teaching he acknowledges his failures and learns from them, he pushes his students and works from the soul space. But also works from the heart space, he is rarely annoyed with students and can tolerate a lot and yet many leaves and go with other teachers and I'm not saying these teachers are wrong I am telling you this as many are right, but some are better than others. Always stick with a good teacher who can watch you growing, aim to make you better than them, are that stage in your development and remember learning is a life lesson, your cup is never full.

This teacher I know from watching him teach is working from the contract as per lifetime is a higher-level soul. And yet has learnt many lessons from others he teaches. Never be afraid of learning more and changing your opinion on what you didn't know before. Many of you will have worked in the higher realms with him. And many will have worked with him here in this lifetime. I will give no more, but this is what many of the teachers we see in your lifetime should aspire to be like. Changing and changing again to allow growth, it is but a human failing to stick with one opinion never changing never learning never moving forward. Think before you speak or in our author's case she channels many in a day and says a lot of humour things before she realises she has said them, it's the personality of a soul. However, she doesn't think, and higher guides do not get it. A lot of hard lessons learnt, and many of you are the same, we come to teach, and we come to assist in life."

**Jacob:** "There are no favourites and yet we jolly you along when you are down, it is imperative you know your team in this lifetime. Espically if you are working with us, you do not need to ask our names, but you can assign names to us based on the energy around us you feel, having a name gives familiarity, and through that, it's easier to know us."

"Learning your thoughts from ours, if you do not know just simply ask. We never lie to you, and we always ask that you learn to recognise silence from the mind, you are not always open to spirit, but you are always there. Learn the differences. Drinking water instead of juice helps the brain stay rehydrated when working and yet many channelers do not work through the direct thought process we skip that part, star seed guides work solely on telepathic speak, whereas spiritual world guides work through you when channelling. What are the main differences when working with the higher guides? Now not all higher guides are star seed and so on but the majority of them are. So, when someone tells you their guide is a higher guide be respectful of them. When your guide comes through and tells you he/she, they are a higher guide or guardian they are star seed. Not alien this is disrespectful, and yet I hear the Author when she worked with Dean, she called him an Alien guide she wasn't wrong, but didn't know the differences then like now."

"It's all about learning, and in truth, he was quite rude and **MF** who had taken her there was also as bad. His temperament as a higher guardian from another world couldn't pick up the joke, however watching the Author for as many years as he had I thought it amusing. We often joke here too; do not think we are how do you put it? Stuck up we are far from it.

Immortality and living forever would be awfully boring without some fun. Dean Is waiting in the wings to come to wind up our Author he gets on well with her now, though in the earlier channels you can see the differences where they argued a lot. It's all fun and personality clashes and learning to know. So much so your Author sought out reading from a guardian asking if what Dean was giving was in-fact real. Well, he is back again so you know it was just confirmation when one sees and hears another being for maybe the first time you can only expect confirmation to be sought out."

**Jacob:** "Good day to you Author I will seek out your company again soon."

**Author:** "*Thank you, Jacob it was lovely you hear and see you again.*"

# 5

# STAR SEED AND INNER AND OUTER DIMENSIONAL TRAVEL

**Author:** *After having a reading with Trance Medium Elaine Thorpe, and her Guide Jonathan. He backed up my work with the Inner and Outer Dimensions.*

**Zealon:** Good afternoon my dear we met yesterday while you were receiving your reading with the lovely Jonathan, Zealon I'm called.

Yes, your correct It is me that sends you to bed when you're tired, you're not tired, yet we will have a little chat before you are called away, and again when you come back.

Working and living in the higher dimensions, and other planets. We all have worlds within worlds, dimensional worlds and this is what we were conveying to Jonathan yesterday. We wish to impart some information for your studies and channelling working with us is extremely important. And while many are connected to us many do not work with us, we have no telepathic connections that are able to channel the word correctly. Dr M was with you only shortly, and he was giving information regarding channels, do you have any questions regarding this form of communication over the telepathic work we do? I ask because the telepathic connections to our world have broadened the mind of yours, making this much easier for your own spiritual world to connect this way moreover the channelling.

**Author:** *I only ask not for me but for others a friend was checking in recently and said she felt she was being influenced and this sparked my interest. When this goes out, many will step forward and claim they are working this way and are being "influenced." can you see this happening and or does it happen?*

**Zealon:** Yes, I see where you're coming from Author. I almost called you by name. I see that now you're connecting this for your book.

Now I can give you this Author, no we not *Never Influence other beings.* It's a rule of the council; we live by a code of conduct if you like, not so much in the written rule it's integrity we all have, we never would influence others. When it's in your future to connect to us; the connections are made slowly so let's just say it like this, look at your own story. If we have tried to connect on a telepathic connection, we wouldn't have been able to first and foremost your mind couldn't handle the connections, as the neutrons in the brain as the physical part of the brain. Needs to get used to the energy needed for certain parts of the human brain, to be used for this work. Second the consciousness of the human we are connecting to needs to be elevated to a degree, we just cannot slip in there without some level of impact to the mind. The impact being headaches, mad thirst. Our energy affects the physical part of self, the self that is alive in the world. I have no doubt your friend is not being influenced by us.

**Author:** *Yes, I have a list of questions in my mind. Do you want to work on them before we work on your list?*

**Zealon:** Yes, that is good we can do that if you write it here and we can work through them.

**Author:** *How does your family systems work if the world in which you're from is predominantly male? The male/male relationships that are not easily accepted on our world and I was told that basically, we would as an Earths people will not be allowed into other worlds unless this is sorted, please elaborate surely this is not the main reason?*

*Doctors of your worlds have many medicines that would help our world can you give me something on them. Am I talking and chatting with "Dead or Living beings in other worlds" or guides from other worlds or both, can you explain?*

**Zealon**: As you know I am from another time in space, I'm a guide but not a "Dead" guide by your standards. I can tell your mind is a little troubled in understanding this, as we can be connected via the telepathic mind. And not as your spiritual world guides, they allow us the connections to their incarnated souls based on the mind, and lifetimes they are living. Take your lifetime this lifetime for example. We are connecting I'm in another dimensional world, or universe you know how the energy works your auric field is universal, and we tap into this via our universal mind, oh alright allow me to give an example, I'm sure this is one of yours so allow me to use this again for you- from our point of view. Our minds connect to the mind of the open channel energetically connected- to the mind of the medium. Look around you we can "see" more than the human mind can perceive, as we see very differently to you from the outer dimensional time in space.

Your soul lights are just that, soul lights, very like your Auric field is the heartbeat of your universe. We connect to this energy and almost zero in on the mind of the incarnated soul, and yes you can connect to us very easily if the lines of communication are already opened. As you called for Dean, I Know many of you will not understand this, and this is very much alright. Only the some will connect the dots and know its correct; it's not a new connection just a new way of describing it.

You see the blackness around you imagine standing in a dark room, very black and seeing nothing not even your hand if you lifted it, so it was your hand in front of your face it's that dark, that's the universe. Now imagine the soul lights bright and pulsing against the universe, this is the chart we have to work within the mind, our mind and through this, we know who you are via our connections to you. We have worked and lived with all of whom we connect to, it's a soul connection, and as we are connected to each incarnate being who has lived with us here and other planets-it will be that way throughout all of your lives. We know you by your energy, we know you by your soul lights. This is how your soul knows we talk truths.

Our family systems are like yours and not. We are born as a soul like yourselves and though you are only understanding of your own biology, let me try to explain some of ours as not all worlds are the same. Earth world is as far away from any other of our worlds as it gets, Sex is not just for pro-creation on your world, and yet on ours, it is. We connect via the mind and through feelings and love this way. Yes, we hug and yes, we have contact with others through procreation is very different in our worlds. Many of us are having both male and female, like your tree frogs, this is how we pro-create but none of us "give birth" all of our young on our planet is cloned if you like. Though not so, as I'm trying to give the best of my ability to your own understanding, some are genetically cloned the best workers the most prowess. Abilities and understanding of the biological seeding of our world is best done by bringing in the Dr of life who works across many universes. Let me answer other questions then I will allow him to come to give you some off-world examples of biological life. Some "males" do have young, but some just carry seed that needs to be taken and grown on, in the medical facilities we have on our planets. Again, the Dr of Life will explain.

Author, how can we allow you to live off your own world if you cannot embrace differences in your own world. (*I don't mean you personally*) We see the damage daily that the human does to their own, our world is male all male, and we love each other, we respect we have our families and a community there is no fighting no ego and no rules, and yet we live and live good. This hate you all have for people of your own worlds one side over another, and so on, this is why we will never allow you to find our worlds. Let alone leave your own galaxies. Many of the humans on your world are embracing of differences and change, many of you are living your best lives while other are waking up. We have many different races across the galaxies and into outer regions of other planets, and yet your world is the most polluted the most damaged, and yet each and every Earthly year it's getting worse. Medically scientifically every way that matters it's getting worse.

Please our main objective for coming to your world for interacting with you as a people, is to help your world by documenting- all "We" can with you and Others. We will allow the knowledge to be passed from one to the other we are allowing for the people who will not believe and will never understand, as this is not their paths. But we give the information that even if it's not understood in your lifetime, ascetically it will be believed, as the mind is a powerful tool Author the mind will catch up in some generations. And while we make use of what we have, we will continue to teach you throughout your earthly life because it's for the betterment of your species.

It doesn't matter that you're not trained in sciences, or Medicines as our world is predominantly different to yours more forward, much more intelligent and much more than anything you have. And it's not being told to make the peoples of the earth feel less than, it's because you will never as a planet gets to where we are. The human body can simply not break down this for yourselves. We have sat on our hands for many generations and watched you struggle for yourselves. The intelligent mind doesn't believe in God; it closed off to believe in other worlds- other lives - on other worlds, so the minds that could understand the challenges of your own world vs our worlds are closed to us.

And the minds that are open to highly intelligent beings from other worlds are close to that of the sciences and medical advancements, and it's not because one is "not" intelligent the channeller and the telepathic mind of the human is far more intelligent he just doesn't understand why. He simply can not understand the workings of the machinery or the sciences in which he will bring, or she in this instant because the brain is developed differently from that of the "*Earthly scientist.*"

I'm going to introduce you to the Doctors and Scientist you will be working with tomorrow earth time, we need to get you on track with this. And though we have all the time in the world, yours and ours we know of your schedule compared to the spiritual world, which is respectfully wanting to send in a Doctor of medicine and other things to work with us and you also. Now please we know your names policy for this is simply doesn't matter. We are coming in via our own names as we are Dimensional.

Doctor Zyban, from the Pleiadeans, He is a doctor of life and all living animal and us alike. Would it help if we called us People? Or beings Author?

**Author:** *People or beings, Zealon it will never matter.*

**Zealon:** Then we will stick with our beings because we do not feel that people are what we are, we are higher beings. We have no collective name we only use our own names. Orion's, Pleiadeans etc. so we will go with this or beings.

We have up **Doctor Seraphor**, Welcome Doctors. Seraphor is a doctor or a manipulator of energy and auric fields in all beings.

**Author:** *Sorry to interrupt I'm not sure I'm going to remember these names, Zealon.*

**Zealon:** Of course, you will be my dear we will tell you who we are when we speak with you.

**Author:** *Alright that's fine, is Dean coming too?*

**Zealon:** No not tomorrow unless you request him, he is busy.

**Author;** *That's fine I'm alright I will suss this out, Energy has a Doctor and not a scientist?*

**Zealon:** Doctors on our planets, worlds and dimensions are different to your own on your own world. We have many specialists in all areas, we call them Doctors because they specialise in many things. We have as you can see I'm showing to your we have the ships doctor who manipulates the energy we tap into as we travel across the dimensions. Now imagine your own Jetstream Author, this is similar to the Energy we connect to while travelling we lower the vibrational pull on the ship and align ourselves within the world we which to travel to, and then that's is, faster than the speed of light and almost to the speed of thought, now measure that out and this is how fast we are getting from here to there.

When a being presents to the Energy Doctors with a little energy off-kilter many other things can go wrong because of this misplacement of energy. We do not wish this to go wrong.

**Author:** *Why didn't we continue?*

**Zealon:** We had to wait until your energy stabilised again and now, you're ready so I will bring in the doctors to work now.

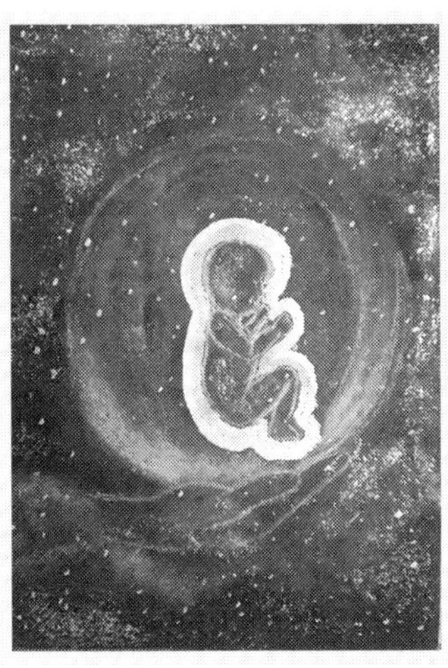

*Star-seed soul Channelled and painted by psychic artist and Medium, Lee-Anne Higgs.*

## Off World Doctors. Life in all Dimensions. And Dr of Energy Manipulation.

**Dr Z.** A SPARK THAT'S ALL IT TOOK, ONE SPARK IN THE universe and that is how all life was formed, life begins and ends the same way. Particles of life that can be seen with the human eye and can be seen from our point of view and of course if you see and feel the energy, you feel the first sparks of life, this is how we begin. We carry that spark within us, many of our race carry the ability to seed that spark both within one, two the seed and the spark and thus begins the start of life on our world, many worlds differ from yours. And I can just say. It's only the human beings like you that do; many procreate so much differently. We are children of the universe, and this is energy all life is energy, and as our minds are connected to the whole, it is only fair to presume that this is the way one begins their life.

The biological system to all beings is fundamentally different. We love we connect on a much deeper level, mind to mind and body to body through the mind. We have these differences, and they are different. We are different from your human. Humanity is a rare form you care, and so do we. You love, and yet we do also on a fundamentally higher charged connection. Than that of body to body. Mind to mind.

Soul self to soul self, all of us are connected on a soul level all of our worlds are soul partners. We have free will in the higher dimensions, and these are the dimensions that are like your world only this way. Pro-creation isn't physical always; we know where each other is by connecting to the mind. Merging self with self. Love is the backbone of many societies and yet comes in different ranks for others. Family systems while they work in many worlds, we have limited family on our world, we have a primary parent and another who is chosen from the soul connection who raises young ones. As the seed soul is born or created from the main parent the primary might carry, or they might be in an artificial womb or basin, like your own and artificially fed with the needs of the body. When the child or young one is released from the main primary being, and the soul connection or parent will raise them. Or they will join the main nursery until ready to interconnect to the main body of the ship, we grow different and live longer so few young ones are created compared to your world.

Now we move to the Greys Orion, and otherworldly beings have Greys but so do many other planets. And worlds, so your probably wondering biology their too, it's so very simple again what your world calls A-Sexual. Many of the worlds are Androgynous and prefer to be called male. They are a predominately male society- this has always been this way and weather and time, or should I say atmospherically many are chosen this way. It's always been and not as your world would wonder why no females. No females are needed in this world.

Now we move to the red planet you know this world Author, this is a world similar to your own and yet not. As you know, procreation is the same as your world very physical and sex for procreation is mainly this way. That said Author bonds of family run deep in this world. Bonds of love run deep male to male, female to female and Androgynous. Gender is not as much of discussion as your world; the body is able for one or other or many. The Body though resembles human, is much more the lungs are well developed there is no need for the many miles of gut and intestines as they eat ever so little, the body and muscle are more defined, and the ego is none existent, And yet a world within a world.

The bobo plant is their main diet, of course, it's a small name given to the plant the longer name I will give when we give the flora details, it basically means staple. It acts as a filler if you like, these beings connect and live mainly by energy and a few foodstuffs. They do not need oil the world is adapted to living with the energy around the planet the nebula of that world, while a pain for science it is a massive help. With the preservation of energy, the higher end sustainable energy comes from the centre of the nebula; this is the thicker or denser energy that causes many to struggle with signals in and out of the world. The males are the main producers of family here with females less they make up most of the scientists on this planet. As the mind of the female seems to be able to connect better to the plant life of this world knowing when to harvest via the energy connected to the heart self. The males of their species seem to be able to tune in to the base energy of the planet, and rock faces. The denser the rock face, the better the male energy can penetrate the energetic system. The difference in male and female energy is not a lot, but slight- and yet is so very different that they utilise this to live better between self.

Let me take you back to Orion, mainly a water planet and a crystal city. Many young ones are raised in a nursery system while parents are taken in and out of the city to work. When older they are training in the ships of the world, they specialise in rocks and crystals and animals, and these are the adventures. They are so deeply spiritual they are born with the knowingness of ones, and that deep connection to the universe. All core memories and energetically connected to the world around them. The closest you will see ever to these beings are the beings of your fictitious world the Avatar film. We rejoiced when we were made aware of this by Dean your friend and guide, he was optimistic your world had made the connection and yet you seemed to know this was fictitious and left it at that. And yet Orion and some of the smaller species of beings are living like that. Not so fictitious now Author huh!

Connected to the water the trees the animals all energy based. We are as beings connected to the universe in which we all live and come from. All of us, and while many of us specialise in something it is but a lifetime to live and learn.

The harder by far lifetimes are your own. You're all so interested in getting off your own planet, and yet you know nothing of ours, and yet you know nothing of the power of your own minds, many of you have the power to connect and talk to each other across the miles, and yet you do not. And many of you have the power to talk to us, and so few do. Author many in your small circle of workers have the power to connect to their own spiritual worlds, and yet they do not they connect only on the physical level and may not even that way.

The Pleiadeans are also a procreator being that creates using the same physical system but so very different. And yet they too use cloning as do many of us. It's "the same but different" this is a saying I think one of your spiritual guides used at the beginning of Alive and free. Predominately they look human and yet have few differences they hear much better the internal hearing system is far widely advanced compared to the human body. They hear sharper low dense noises from the internal hearing is as different from them as we are to us.

The eardrum is larger, and the bones are almost feather-like structure, very fine it is like rubbing two unicorn hairs together, they are that fine. They have a fine circulatory system within the body the veins are finer, and their hearts have five chambers, not four. And they have a collection of nerves around the heart that enables the feeling of self to be broad, their internal body of vitals, sharper than that of the human system. The thoracic system is less dense in terms of bone structure, and the lungs have a larger alveolar system making it easier to breath. They have no gallbladder, but they do have a liver similar to humans, that filters toxins from the body. They breathe in and they digest different from the human, their colon and the intestinal system is vastly different.

It's almost awkward explaining to you author we need to do a whole body internal structural document, and we will I'm just giving you brief of the Pleiadean right now though we will do all of the transdimensional beings we will work with. You have a brief connection with Dean about the way he sees, and we need to do one for all, the Pleiadean, sees but their optical nerves are way stronger than that of the human they see through the mind that connects to the nerve in their eye. And projects out to others the vision they see, so not only do they "see" but anyone they are connected with on a higher plane is also seeing. Objectively what they see with their eyes.

If it's alright with you, we have no set "allowed" and not allowed here I'm going to give you many biological systems of many of our beings and animals. You would be surprised; I know your own mind has no references for these animals so we will show you also. We showed Dolores also, and she was well let's just say surprised covers it.

## The spiritual world, with Havern.

**Author:** *I just read there are no buildings in Heaven and yet I have been channelling guides in buildings around buildings etc. so how is it one guide says no, and one guide says yes, surely, it's a yes or a no, or has the channel got it wrong as many do?*

**Havern:** Oh, dear Author you seem to have stumbled upon a bad channel, or a guide in a separate generational spiritual world or let's just say a spiritual world not consistent with the "Normal" world in which we live.

**Author:** *Eh, Come again.*

**Havern:** Alright, remember we told of other worlds other heavens other spiritual worlds, remember this yes?

**Author:** *Yes,*

**Havern:** We I felt we must be clear on this for your work, some of the main reason's channels get mixed up is there are many levels to the spiritual world and in each "world" or planet a World within a world. Many Parallels and many more the mental worlds the physical worlds the imitation worlds all thrive on energy. So yes, these worlds are levels of consciousness-energy and of soul level selves.

For example, the Newer souls, the newborn souls who come from their incarnations- from other worlds and planets. They do not know all of life resides in the world you would for example. Your soul growth is exponentially higher than that of new souls, now we have guides and guardians for every level of the spiritual world, even the lower levels, and it's in these levels you will find no buildings or other spiritual worlds each world is on its own merits or what they feel is right. The mediums and metaphysical minds and soul are in the worlds that manifest what is needed to be utilised by self for learning reasons. The Libraries the healing rooms the healing fountains, many other parallels have none of these, and the same goes for some part of the Animal kingdom, and the Red planet has healing rooms, but no teaching library's no higher realms. Do you understand now Author?

**Author:** *Yes. So, the channel never made a mistake? He was simply working with a guide from these stations if you like; or like it has been said before.*

*So, what about other planets souls are they contracted to live in the spirit world, here this one, when I was reading a channel about my own contract, they said my homeworld was destroyed, and I was anchored to the spiritual world, are there other reasons why one would be anchored to another planet?*

**Havern**: We will work with your soul contract it's an easier one to remember for me.

Let's say yes your planet is rendered lifeless, and we

know this to be correct, though it's still there we are working on here to work out a new eco-system. She is just an example of what free will cause, the beings from Sirius teamed with another outer planet and caused this chaos many millennia ago. You would know this is your higher form, this question wouldn't come up, but then we couldn't use you to write the book either. So, continue.

When the first contact was made from the earth world to call out for help from the twelve, you were still incarnated upon the earth world and had been for many lives.

If I remember it was around the time of the 1930s so not really that long ago, however, what you won't remember if this has happened before, many aeons of time ago when the ice age was over the planet you were working on the call came from the higher realms to populate a new world.

We had to place guides guardians' higher souls on with newer souls, it was to be a free will world, so we opted for many to come, along with the planets own evolving state of mammals. The ones who have been evolving and living in her own world, these are of course spiritual world souls born, and then add the star seeds the consciousness of the planet grew exponentially. And much faster than if they were left alone to evolve.

However, each star-seed soul couldn't be simply left to incarnate alone we knew they would have a backup if you like. A plan of action and yet you called for them to be picked up by your own people, now come on I know you know where this is going. But the only trouble is with the human mind it doesn't understand the backup plans, and the contracts made. I know I am making us sound clinical here Author, but we are really not, your era your planet your guides, guardians in the making are explorer souls. You test life on other planets to enable you to incarnate you wanted to anchor some souls on the spiritual world, and we agreed.

Now into this "Project if you like the planet of your own was made inhabitable, and many star seeds came to Earth and that there is your second home. Though a denser energy planet, the souls made teachers and sailors, storytellers and scientists Authors and many more aside the drawback are the human body is not suitable for the energy around your souls and or your etheric body if you like. So, you falter easier your body dies faster, and you return to spirit much faster than the "spiritual world" original soul.

The Aliens who are star-seed souls, keep a check on the lives of the souls, in the human body, pro-creation using the DNA of mixed planetary beings and injecting into the human, we know all that goes on Author even in this body you don't not this life, but you do. And this is where the many sides to the human dulled mind don't understand; they too are star-seed, many souls are from far-flung planets.

The call to arms if you like from other guides to incarnate to the earth world to waken them to the power of the universe has been hard on them, they are not learning as fast as we would like, they are killing themselves Author, and really this book no any others won't change that. They are changeable via generations, so the next two are important, and the one after that will be worth reincarnating for. I know I know that this is another "science-fiction" channel and yet it's a channel that is needed to be heard, Author as a Contracts guide, I have seen just about every soul coming asking for a lifetime of learning and shock and awe and yet how many fail because they are caught up in the "Human" facade. Too many are all.

Many souls are anchored in the spiritual world it

means the same to each soul, it means you can learn from each angle each lifetime, and even the anchored part can continue to do the jobs you require, for example, yours and Rhaji's lives.

Rhaji's guides this lifetime with you, waiting for you.

Let's have him in here for you, while we are speaking the truth and hard hitting's.

I'll not go too far we have more work. Here he is ...

**Author***: Alright just don't shout at me again.*

**Rhaji:** Hello my friend and twin, how are you?

**Author:** *Really? I suppose I'm alright as far as this goes but I would appreciate a better life I suppose. I feel swamped and not in a good way, sore back human life dragging me down, I just want to be left alone to channel and chat to home, tell me Rhaji did we really just come here for this. As it seems like the biggest thing I have ever done and yet I Feel like I'm working with a blindfold and one hand behind my back.*

*Tell me what can be changed to make it so?*

**Rhaji:** Really you feel like that? Okay don't answer I know you do, then first and foremost yes, we did come here just for that, and to help others I know the human you, is dragging it down, I understand that. So, there is not a lot one can say about that scenario; only it will get better, but I understand that you could say really when? You go back to the homeworld I'll still be here feeling like this, so no I'm not going to say it, but what I Will say is this, yes, this the life path. We fought to do this, used all of life's experiences to point to do this, yours and mine. And as a writer in other lives we utilise my experiences, and as a medium and a trance medium we utilise yours, but as an Altered state we utilise this; the compartmentalisation is to occupy and box up and place out of the way so we can work.

It's taken time to train this with you, it seemed oh like it would never get there, but we know from here we can show your life will be getting better simply because we needed you incapacitated if you like, to sit and write, you couldn't do it on the run now could you.? First and foremost, we had to make a choice. Hard times are hard and become harder, but it's the human life, then we can work on the soul's experiences of the human life.

We also need to consider the help you came for, others not just you,

**Author:** *So why aren't they suffering like I am? How they gonna learn from this when someone keeps rescuing them..?*

**Rhaji:** When you're no longer willing to rescue them, they will learn to stand on own or fall, it's just that simple.

**Author:** *Surely, it's their contract failing, not mine. Jeepers for once I want it to go well is all...*

**Rhaji:** I will see what we can do from here. Havern has said his part, and yes, we will help a lot more and now can you see why we didn't opt to come together this time, and no time this is it I wanted to guide. These books you can do yourself only then you won't hear "Don't you Dare" as you change a word.

I will say this one more time because its warranted, you feel because I feel, you see because I see and I Love because you do. This is for all twin flames, so please try and pick yourself up this is why I'm around a little more, I know much will come from this Author, much a lot actually will come we admire the stubbornness and pride in using the brain, and being able to channel in all situations and **MN** and **DC** Proved that for us recently we will be bringing **MN** soon again to work he is very interested in off-world he won't incarnate for a while. And certainly not since he discovered off world ideals, and he is working with star-seeds and off-world, and life between life work it will go into the archives for all to read from there and here,.

Remember I said this Author, trust only those you know now.

## Ascension twin flames.

**Author:** *If one is in the spiritual world, the consciousness being a lot higher than that of the twin incarnated, will the twin ultimately higher the consciousness of the human body of which they inhabit at the point of the incarnation?*

**Rhaji:** Yes, Author (Smiles)

We are not too far away subconsciously measured, though the human body is dulling the strength of the connection somewhat, when you "get out" you and I will level up to whichever connection is highest, we will not be unlevel if that's what you're thinking.

Yes, Author, the awakened soul needs less dream-state learning through the body, does tend to tire more if your star-seed. Reason being as we stated before the body of the star-seed tends to fail faster due to the higher energy around the soul. And the Etheric body.

## The Others.

**Dr H:** When the moon landings took place the other side of the moon was inhabited by us the others. Feel the energy we bring with us it's a tight energy Author we will try and level this out for you, so you do not feel like you do right now.

The dark side of the moon they call it.

We inhabit a lot of the moon we also have satellites in the Stratosphere around your world; we have the Hubble set to see what it is we require your people to see. A lot is going on outside of your own planet that they do not wish for you to see and we are not here to blow the whistle on them. We need to set the record straight with the incarnated souls upon your Earth world.

This earth world of yours was created by us, with help from the souls upon your spirit world, the dimensional shifts made it possible we could all work together in total secrecy and with the needed energy to build a world and ecosystem. Your higher guardian Jacob is one of your top ecosystem guides. He helps with that and when he calls us in and lets us know the Earth world is heading for trouble we listen.

We will only ever get involved if needs are, we always said this at the beginning of all things. However, no matter what has been seen to come to pass we have only needed to step in and send crafts to step in a handful of times throughout your histories and one of the times was Fukushima as this too has been recorded and then cover files disappear. We do not have anything to do with your world if we can possibly help it.

This has changed of late as many as seventy earth years- have passed since we became involved again in your world, we were always there we are now actively involved with the pollution problems around the globe, from simple tasks to larger oceanic tasks, you pollute the Earth you pollute the waters. The oceans are dying the animals are suffering, and the science is off the charts, but your leaders want to charge more $ for this, it's a never-ending circle of a disaster waiting to happen.

WE HAVE BEEN SENDING CRAFTS OF OUR SCIENTISTS TO your world, various states and countries and small cities around your world to test waters soil, and air. We have taken samples and animals to look at we have taken many samples across the board. We have been watching your weather and knowing what we know one would believe this is deliberately being set from labs across the globe.

The weather anomalies some cities are experiencing are interfered with anomalies, not all. Now that you have taken to interrupting nature you want to play god. You wish to lower the population by natural ways, that others will not notice.

Testing vaccines and chemicals in your own world is another reason we get involved. You might see our ships you might see there is a pattern to our comings and goings. If you see us know we mean you no harm. We work with others from other worlds all designed to help the Earth world.

Your world was deliberately set across the universe away from other inhabited planets as the others do not have the free will your world has, and we do not have the ego your world has and our life on these planetary systems are running and flourishing in their worlds much better than your own.

Out of the other worlds, some do have free will, NON-have ego it's not our way. On these worlds, we have set up a test system a graph if you like data collected from your Earth world and now you can see why we are worried enough to make our presence known.

We wish to make it known to you all we are around and will continue to be so until there is a monumental effort made to curtail the damages done, it's not looking good for a lot of life on your planet.

**Author:** *Can we change the damage? Or what if anything can stop it or is it too late?*

**Dr H**: Firstly, no you cannot change it. The human is self-sacrificing their own ecosystem in favour of total nothingness, they do not care for the generations behind them, and sitting celebrities down in a hall while congratulating them on work started to help stop this problem is not helping, it's not hindering, but it's not helping either.

Next stopping this, yes it can be stopped/slowed if the collective persons in power can look at the data from the scientific minds across the globe and the data we too have supplied. And advising that all carbon and coal and energy resources be changed. Stopped and moved on giving an amount of time and never worry about cost. Because the cost to the planet it much higher than the monetary cost it would, to stop burning coal, stop burning and using other carbon items into the atmosphere. Carbon fissure in the rock surfaces, breaking up the sea floor and burning oil and natural gases, fracking is causing rock fractures across fault lines aggravating earthquake issues, and while they are not showing in your graphs, they show in ours. Burning gases that are both dangerous to the human lungs but to the animal and the others who live so far away you have no measurements for us, we too are registering the issues from our side of the universe.

We will come to the Pharma companies later, while it's not our problem we have much to say on that subject also.

You wonder how we survive on the surface of the moon? We are not affected by the gravitational pull that the human is, we are not affected by many of the same, we are affected more or not at all.

We live subterrestrial upon the Moon; we do not live on the Dark side; the term was coined back in the day so they couldn't see us. Or so they wouldn't show our bases to the earth dwellers as we called them back then, they believed there would be anarchy in the streets if they thought the general public of your world, knew we lived upon the Moon. They thought that we would attack, the problem is the earth dwellers are confrontational beings, and if they do not understand it, they blow it up. An Earth is saying, and I get into bother on my home planet for saying it all the time.

I picked it up on your planet.

I said it to my superior about the Earth dwellers; I said why do they not treat us like dogs, (*kick soil over us and piss on us and walk away*). Now I knew what I was telling him; he did not. I got into much bother for that remark, He now understands.

We wish only to be left alone; we do not wish to wage wars with the planet we helped to make, because the inhabitants are happily living in the here and now and some believe only what the governments have told them.

Living under the planet as opposed to the earth side of the moon, we are not seen, we are not bothered about until photos of the moon with our bases on are shown. We will not live in darkness because some humans cannot believe we exist. We are your government's biggest lie to date along with 9/11 of course.

So, if they can do that to their own people. I do not need to say any more. The strongest country in the world is the USA basically because of its size.

**Author:** *You do not have a good outlook on pollution, if you are annoyed about the celebrities helping, so what if they sit around at least they are trying to empower.*

**Dr H:** No Author they are patting themselves on the back for bringing it to light.

**Author:** *I do not agree with you here, and I might be channelling you, I haven't got to agree with you. I think you're very harsh. Also, the scientists here on the Earth, our scientists are helping with statistics etc. I don't know enough to argue this out with you only lots are going on in other countries to help. Some of the celebrities are at the forefront of the work being done regarding getting rid of the carbon* *footprints, and about bringing fracking to the homes of the people who wouldn't know anything otherwise, I think it's very unfair of you to blame them for doing nothing when they are doing plenty. I'll shut up now. I'm done arguing with Guardians and guides, and I am not starting with Others.*

**Dr H:** I agree I was harsh. It doesn't make any difference whether they are celebrities or governmental officials, the truth of the matter is- nothing is doing that's stopping this anytime soon.

Now let's move on.

**Johan:** I called on the others to come to take a look at the state of your world many Earth years ago, due to the animals that were returning home in the droves to pollution, many of that being oil spills and still topping the bill across the USA Is oil spills. Author, you have seen how the government officials have strong-armed the indigenous peoples of the USA and put pipelines across their lands. We have to agree with the indigenous peoples this is going to keep on keeping on unless its stopped. Also, the chances of the leaking pollutants into drinking water was high during the fights of the last five-ten years, and I hate to say it again, but they were correct many souls will be returning home from a natural disaster that is waiting to happen upon your earth world from pollution.

Fracking in Wales in the UK, fracking in the USA and in Australia should and will all be banned. It's been creating multiple problems across the globe. How long to the Humans consider they can get away with rape of the natural world?

## Vaccines of the children.

**Dr H:** Selenium in vaccines, in all vaccines works to

the benefit on some, not to others the detrimental effects are not seen for many a while, the bother your world has is that it seems to be good with working with what-ifs rather than the now.

They do not stop to wonder if they should.

**Dr H:** While as Others, Ets or Aliens whoever like to call us we are not about testing on our own, and while some vaccines I'm sure are not Bad as per, I would like to test the vaccines they give to your young on the young of the developer.

Your cancer treatments all well and good as they are wouldn't be needed if you looked at why cancer is as prevalent in the human species as it is. One of your doctors made a very good point, he likened the body and lungs of the Human of that of a filter and stated the pollution pumping into the air each day is not meant to be filtered out like that around the body, hence the cancers and illnesses seen in the human are also seen in pets. We agree with him.

Our Wish for your World is of this; your pollution habits are changed, you make use of the free energy around your planet. You make use of not just the solar energy but that from water also. You get shot of the cars that drink diesel and dangerous gasses, and you reinvent your world while you still have one to work with.

None of your religions will save you if you do not. In fact, none of your religions will save you anyway, even praying won't help. For its when no help comes, they complain about their false gods. For actions speak much louder than praying about it.

We understand that "*God*" the universal creator the divine energy aka the Devine. Can be collectively prayed too and it will work as the universal energy works for you and with you. The power of negativity coming from around your planet, your planet your world has bad mental health. Negative Earth.

Positively is what we need from the Earth dwellers. And the promise of adjustment or there will be no Earth to incarnate too, and that is a promise from Us to you. I will leave now and leave your Author to continue on her path for this book, thank you for channelling us. It is the mind you have, that will help when we come back again.

Thank you Author it was a pleasure. Even when you told me off. *(Dr H, smiles)*

## How one guide describes working with humans, and a misunderstanding.

**Soratola:** The word I think is good evening is it not author?

**Author:** *Yes, you are correct, I don't know who I am chatting with right now, so I will just ask this, what am I being told here that is not something I haven't already been told. I know the Off-world guides coming through have a reason for this, I know that your all working with the lightworkers right now.*

**Soratola:** Lemurians hybrid Vega, Author, have you ever wondered why you are being shown the hieroglyphics on your bedroom wall of late?

**Author:** *You know I have, and Jonathan said it's the messengers. Amongst other things.*

**Soratola:** Then forgive me while I correct you, we came to the Earth world to build pyramids the earth is just another planet we have inhabited throughout the solar system, there are and where many wars around your planet and ours and virtually every planet within the galaxies. Each planet has their own armies if you like, warriors soldiers their own military forces, each force protects their planet and others we have been advised to protect. We have a system on each world seen from way into the atmosphere of that world where we are a Map if you like, this we didn't have on your world. Around the time of the gods in Egypt and Greece, we covered Asia and China, and we inhabited many countries and continents your world is just a world, nothing special but somewhere we can live, or could live should I say.

We also lived with the gods these came from our world and others, we build the pyramids and the great cities below, where many of our people still live, your world is cloaked in secrecy it always has been the shadow governments run the governments and the people that get in the way are simply no more. Again, we lived with Ria the sun god, the god of life and many others. The Spartans were trained to protect our ways and protect the earth from many of the alien races coming to the earth when they were fighting, they didn't know who they were fighting, only the many of reptilian forces where Spartans, many greys and other energy manipulators, where within these walls. We never interfered we let them, and when our people were tired of this planet many moved on, however, we have a big connection to the USA, and many other countries, like China and Asia. We were a fighting force that came here to build, and we were never meant to stay.

In these early days, the scripture was that of the hieroglyphics, these hold true for many of our peoples many still work this way. We left many hints and tips of who we were around your planet, we foresee a time when the world was at peace, and yet it's as far away from peace now as it was then. The human has been killing our kind and working on our kind like lab rats for many of your years, we have even sent some of our kind and yours to other worlds to live with. Its only strengthened our beliefs we will never be able to live in peace with each other while your world has free will. It gives you a right to do something our kind would never dream of, we hold ourselves in higher regard than that. I am not telling you we were a peaceful force we did what we had to, too survive and yet as many on your world do not even know the world in which they live.

**Author:** *Is it possible we are living parallels daily, it seems our world is well occupied by alien races, and yet many of our kind are oblivious to this happening.*

**Soratola:** No, Author you know why. As many who deny it are these other beings, high in the governments, is where you will find many of these people, they flatly deny who they are because they do not know who they are, and those that do, know this don't want this getting out. However the governments that allow your president to be in the hot seat do not want him to know that the Aliens are a strong force on your world, he cannot hold his own water can you imagine the power he thinks he will hold with this information, no he is a puppet only. Run by a shadow government or secret society, if you like.

Why do you think author many presidents were assassinated over that time? It wasn't because someone didn't like them, they were a threat to security. And many still are, however as the time is drawing closer to the time, we will be revealed we are channelling as many to as much as we can so when this breaks through the "many" will know the truth of their own humanity and what it is to be done.

**Author:** *And what is it to be done?*

**Soratola:** The earth people will rise up and take back their freedom.

**Author:** *Please tell me about the here and the now, what is going on with the revealing of Off-world guides to the lightworkers. It's the first time I have seen you. I don't understand I Know the world is with conflict but why am I asked to do this?*

*If this was only about the people taking back their freedom, why Am I sat here like a noodle channelling this and feeling nothing, or like it's nothing to do with me. I'm not on a strong enough platform to make a difference to this world, Yes, I can agree, and each one agrees makes up more. I do not want to follow blindly I want information that is worth the time or what's my point in all this?*

*You see I understood my point in channelling the guides a look around the spirit world I understood that. I understood the spiritual side of this, but this is entirely off topic for these books, shaking your head at me guides, isn't going to help this. I just do not get it. So, help me out here what am I supposed to be doing with this compared to the spiritual work...*

**Author:** *I lost my wrag with this channel, in the end, it felt pointless. Though over the weekend, I thought about it and decided to continue and got into trouble for shutting them down. I could hear Medium F in my ear the whole weekend.*

## *15.10.18 14.10pm*
## Questions and answers.

**Author:** *Line them up please if you can, I need to channel this stuff, please. Stuff for the book. Time travel backwards. Civilisations. Brains are coming back online etc. Ce5 DNA activation, the lot you know what I'm looking at. Quantum leap evolution.*

**Medium F:** You know they are not amused you shut that down don't you, we warned you they had no sense of humour Author, and you did it anyway.

**Author:** *No, it wasn't down to a sense of humour trust me, and while I Apologise, I will not apologise for not having any understanding of the bigger picture at that time. I Do now, and this came to me in my own time, nothing or no one could have helped, so please continue and they above are my questions, I have been down the proverbial rabbit hole this weekend, and now I am left with* *more questions. I didn't realise their/our programmes were so big it's unbelievable. And yet it feels right to me. So, continue I will take it and not shut no one down, I know you know more than me, so whenever you're ready and remember there are outside influences here.*

**Dean:** Oh Author yes we understand and did from the minute you shut us down, we know as a human the mind is a tool, and it doesn't matter how further forward one's mind is, it needed to come to terms with the telling of something and you did that pretty much straight away, we understand you needed that so never worry and Medium F is just spouting off. .

**Medium F:** Thank you Dean (*Smirks at Dean, our Alien friend*)

**Dean:** So, I am an Alien friend now? I'm just kidding, I know you meant I am an off-world guide, but the alien is not as offensive to me as it was, now I know the context it brought in.

**Medium F:** For our readers at home, Dean was highly offended by the Author calling him an ET guide or Alien, because she was sarcastic and in truth so was, he, this was that the beginning of their earthly relationship, he was offensive she was sarcastic, and now they are friends, no scratch that Family. They are family off-world.

**Dean:** Yes, thank you for that so we must get on, Medium F you can step back now I have it from here, thank you for bringing Her here we must insist that every channel done with a medium their soul is connected to us via their guides, they trust from the spiritual world only this way can they know they are guarded protected and are absolutely channelling a good force. From your question Author, the gas could come from the nebula we have exhausted that in the off-world travel to and from the Red Planet and you remember this channel, it's in both books if

I'm not mistaken. And yes, your help for the book will be along this evening when you start.

The Time portals, Yes absolutely, I can confirm them, yes we do come in via portals we do not burn up in the atmosphere one of us said this the other day I think it was me, we come in via the energy I likened it to the jet stream around your world, and this is a simple way of explaining it, the ships we will explain later as each one is similar but different as per connection to the mind of the one who is at the helm, the Hieroglyphs you see are a direct link to us, and us letting you know we are with you, in the dream state and wakened hour, and while it seems strange to many beings it's not and nor will it ever be, I am your guide you know me, and therefore To be around you is no longer strange you connect reasonably quick but that's only because I am a guide or your guide. My energy is just sitting outside your auric field most times throughout your linear time, and this is another thing we will attempt to explain to you, I know ***EG*** did this in book one.

Interstellar human travel, yes, we have that we are on a programme with the tall whites and Pleiadeans who allow some of the earth's men, to travel through portals to their time frame, live with them access some information and taken back, the human will never be allowed to get beyond their galaxy alone, we do not trust them enough for that. No human trust. They are treating us as lab rats much the same as they do you, however with our species they claim they wait until the body is no longer viable, and yet we do not simply just "Die" our bodies are not made for that, no alien species is just made to die, they do however clone us, and others and mix them with DNA to try to make super-species, your TVs are not wrong in many accepts and You have no idea how pleased we are as a species that you do not watch this invention, it's through this the human is becoming fast a Drone as such, made to work live and pay taxes that fuel much of the "covert" societies behind their "secret space station and programmes" many of their own are blowing the whistle on their own ways of investigating our species.

Again, copy this down here Author so we can refer to your questions without going backwards. Then we will bring ours after your lunch.

Hybrid human yes, they are mixing the DNA of the human with that of the nearest race to them, which would be the Pleiadean and others, they are injecting the embryo into human women and if the child looks "Human" they allow them to keep the child, if not the Government takes the child and the child is given to our kind, to grow on our worlds. Not ours as in mine, others they work with. So Yes, that's happening. Next one conscious ship, yes but you know that anyway, so we bring more at a later date. Let's leave the next DNA activation for now and work on Quantum leap evolution. This is a science that the human has been trying for some time to work out, the linear behind this and no they cannot take what is here and now and move it forward, but there is no need to do that because there are the parallels to this time. Each linear timeline as another slotted into it, for each time you move a cup a key a crystal your adding a timeline, so yes your sitting at this pc channelling me telepathically and yet your still doing that earlier this morning your time because you decided to, it's hard to try to explain to your human mind so let's try another tactic, for each decision you make there is another, so, for example, you decide to go to the shop in the car, but at the last minute you change your mind.

The thought process behind that has it done, and all, the energy behind that thought has gone to the shop, and the here and now is still here again as the energy is behind that thought, I do believe you explained this better in book one with EG than with me here, look at a pack of cards and hold them in your hand, look at the edges of the cards these are all the time signals linear time, is made up of segments sections etc of a thought and an energy, each thought gives it momentum, so you want your van with the prefix add it to that thought put it out there its coming because there is strong energy behind it. It's coming back your making it come bringing it into this reality, see now. I leave this hear its making it work and understanding the processes behind them, Parallels universes work on the same, thought process only with simple changes, there are ley-lines across your world, each ley-line crosses backwards and forwards, into other dimensions, these dimensions are the same as time, each pack of cards each card is a layer a dimension if you like, all made up from the whole, each person is alive in each dimension, and for each decision you give energy too it carries through the dimensions.

There is an Author sitting here writing this it is carrying huge energy behind it, and as you learnt how to close your mind to thoughts and projections, your life is one of the lesser dimensional masses experienced right now, so when the thought process concentrates on only one thing instead of many it makes it more of a reality faster. Do you understand, it almost condenses the energy because it's not spread out over difference dimensions by many thoughts at once.

So, all in all, teaching students to compartmentalize and close down their mind is, in fact, easier for the manifestation of spirit and universal law of attraction through energy.

Nice one Author.

**Author:** *Thank you, Dean, it was a hard do, and I'm glad I learnt I wouldn't be chatting to you otherwise. Please continue.*

**Dean:** Its almost stopping for lunchtime though it's almost evening in your world, right now.

Before we go and leave you for one hour let me say this, you learnt as much as we expected you took over the weekend, because learning this and then coming back to work today gives us much more to play with, we can only play with what's in mind or use what's there to give you a wider scope of what's going on, we work through integrity and always will work this way, the human is corrupt we only agree on a short-term for the human to not allow the civilians of your planet to have total transparency regarding our involvement in the earth world, the human world needs to prepare we are coming here in droves daily and yet your world if blissfully unaware, I am hoping as much as we can this book brings people into an understanding, we want to awaken souls, not keep them oppressed.

This is the human way, not the off-world way. Only then can you embrace your humanity and become who you were created for. The spiritual world is all for the same, so far humanity is on a slippery slope. They will go to great lengths to keep us a secret from your people and we do not understand why, they have been lying over and over about announcing alien life on the earth world for aeons of time and we as a whole collection and something the galactic council agrees on, we are a little fed up. They want our technologies, and we will only share these when humanity knows we exist and are prepared to help you all. Now go for your lunch your physical body is

**Author:** S*tarting again, 16:57 pm.*

**Anzia:** Good afternoon Author I see you are settled now after our chat the last time, I didn't seem to feel you were offended,

**Author:** *I wasn't offended I didn't understand why you were telling me what you did, I do now.*

**Anzia:** Good, what do you feel about the secret space programme?

**Author:** *Well it isn't much of a secret is it? Secret implies no one knows, or no-one outside of the programme themselves knows. We know that to be wrong, so what do you feel we as a human should know about it? I feel I Would like your take on it, your species but more than that I want you to give me what I feel you indicated to Jonathan what you were going to give me, as I know if they are already working on propulsion and as per our discussion with the Off-world doctors. I wonder where now what next?*

**Anzia:** I come from a tiny planet in the solar system of Eurasia this is spelt much different and sounds different but that's what I have for you, We are a small body of Beings, we are very spiritual we believe in the collective consciousness of the one, or the one over all things, one imperial divine force, no divine is not right either but the ultimate energy the creator of all that is. In our world we live subterranean and, on the surface, we have only small rivers and underground springs we ingest planet life ground so only the life energy of the planet is ingested. We waste very little our biology is much different from yours, we are around let me think, see we are not a tall race but I'm learning to explain to you. We are around three and a half feet tall at the grown rate. We grow at an exponential rate compared to many races, and we live for as long as we need to, I know this doesn't give you a lot, but it gives all I'm allowed to give right now. My skin colour is gold this works with the light energy around our world, it's a steady heat, and we are as far from your sun as you are and yet interdimensional, so we do not feel the heat. Also the heat is built within our planet from the many heat sources. We are space travellers, we come to Earth and work with components in technologies, however on your planet we come as peacekeepers we show your world how to grow our foods subterranean, in a compound as such in what is termed north America. We have work with the small greys for making a small craft for them to pilot one to one, this craft is also consciousness directed, from living material.

The grey comes to our world, or we go to theirs we measure their signature for consciousness delivery for the craft they need to work with, this is breathing entity. It's very similar to Artificial intelligence in your world, but not the same either.

Let's say for example he wants to travel to the Pleiades star cluster from our planet, he needs to be able to higher his consciousness let's say ¾ to the moon's energy, and then come in via 72. Ec from Ez: at.s. It will take him where he needs to be. He needs to connect very similar to you would do feel the channel, with him he would need to feel the energy around the craft, feel her pulse and raise that energy level while connecting to the coordinates given when he comes out of the portal he will be able to go via a line of sight to the sector he is looking for, and the same on return.

It's very simple, and we have been building I want to say as it recreates what we do here, but it's not called that at all. Many of the words we give are more complicated however your language does not support this so we give the best we can in all, the implant we use sometimes connects good other times planetary depends on where from, some have a better connection than that of others, so working with the bigger ships the ones where we can carry many of our people and yours, we are reliant on not one connector but two, not all are like this many are one but in the event of one being unable the other can take over we do not make the fighting ships just renaissance ships.

**Author:** *Anzia can you show me around your planet are you allowed to show me some of the work or where you live, do you sleep etc.?*

**Anzia:** We rest yes, nobody can work without the need to rest, we do not have beds as you have but we have resting areas, come I can open your mind to mine, and we can show you our world, now see the over areas, (I *was shown a very futuristic overpass*) you see the shuttle bus like what your earth has, and it's a fibre tube and very light and fast this is our travel for beings like us that do not work in areas like us, these would be for families.

The mountains we have are not mountains they look like them from here you see, (*I do*) They are Pyramids like you have on your world we worked on them too, we were the plotters if you like, map drawers. We pointed the galaxies and led the way in bringing this into existence. Astronomy is relevant on each planet, these light the way from our world to yours via interdimensional travel, we are a forward race, but we do not need too much to survive, we live of course, but we survive on very little.

I am not allowed to show you our homes Author this is why you hit a blank slate with my mind after I showed you the pyramids, I know you understand. We do have nothing to hide our planet is very beautiful, we have more to live outside of this area of inhabited space.

I want to move on to another guide, for now, but not goodbye, we have many more works to do with you for this chapter in your life.

**Dean:** Author I want to bring in Dr Z you had worked with him before he explained the propulsion and planetary shifts to you before now, I step back and let him in.

**Dr Z:** A very good evening to you, Author, I have been watching progress with book one, and we will enforce this and direct more people to it, we realise we need to push these as much as you do, let's push on.

Many of your armies on your world have been relentless and trying to get our technological designs, though we have given some of these up, not enough that can be used against us or used against you. The human is unpredictable, and they have a variety of; how do you say it, well they have a variety of advancements they are keeping from their own people and using it only on the rich, it doesn't matter how they use it for the time being it will not help their rich people, each contract is designed to play out for the rate in which you die, they are off contract for the most part, a lot of the illnesses they many will pass from will have come from our worlds, we are immune to most illnesses though not a lot of human sicknesses can make us sick, however many of ours can make you sick. This is normal is classed as Zoological, many illnesses, we have cures for.

Despite not suffering them on our home worlds we design many, for the human world, planet life solely using flora and fauna, though It doesn't hurt to not offer them for simple reasons, that they do not want us interfering, we do know there will come a time when many of these will be given to your world. Big pharma is held by the rich and people in governments that is mainly the reason we will be investing telling these details to many rather than going through the governments and the united nations, for the most part, these councils want to help the people though they have to work through internal resources we believe it will be too long for the most part before these advancements take off, we do not have many animals that we need to treat on our world, they move in herds and packs and have a raised collective consciousness, able to affect the energy around them, they do not suffer the sicknesses your world does, we do not allow that sort of pollution to invade our soils thus hurting the grasses the animals would ingest.

Our animals feed on plant life that has been grown as a filtration system, like a living filter, they take this and turn it into valuable energy to feed our animals. Nor do we have pets and animals in homes, our lifestyles are very different from you, we are from a star system in the $5^{th}$ dimension, and here there is no way I explain to you in human language our star names, the world doesn't or wouldn't understand it, even if we spelt it out for you. Your words and letters are not like ours. We work on pictures very similar to the Egyptians.

Ask away Author; I will do my best to reply.

**Author:** *What medicines do you have that would have the most impact on prolonging our lives, is it also possible the earth has the technology that can turn back time in the human body?*

**Dr Z:** Yes, and yes. We have enough stockpiled medicine that was developed for the Aids virus that would eradicate it in just two treatments, also depending on the viral load being detectable or not one would do. The medicine called Truvada and Pre-exposure prophylaxis Or PrEP Are one of the same or similar we have better, for the medicine that would eradicate it would wipe it out of the body with no harsh side effects, it totally cleans up the body, this single dose is injectable with the pump action human needle/syringe and thus doing away with the need to take a medicine daily to stop infection, if there is no Aids virus. We are able to do that with many of your diseases. Author for one single moment thinks about this, readers too.

You own the pharma company why would you want a cure, if you can treat patients, that's more money, then every single male in the risk group takes a pill daily, this is a lot of money, whom do you think created the aids virus in the first place Author?

Second yes, there is a capable way to turn back time in the body. Thus the only problem is while on the surface it looks fine the subconscious mind, is libelling to come back, no memories rewritten for a simple fact is DNA memory, and conscious soul memories are stored in the superconscious mind. When the body goes back, the cells and nuclei will start to reformat a faster rate, thus bringing the body back to the time the recreating started. This is a hard process, and while all looks good on the surface, the inner workings of the cells will over time deteriorate this is why we do not mess with time, the human however never asked if they should.

**Author:** *Cancer, and the workings of the moving living bandage the Native doctor was trying to bring in can you tell me if this will be a thing can you give something?*

**Dr Z:** Yes cancer cure is a human body thing, oh alright let me see that is defiantly not what I wanted to say, the human body has the ability to heal from all illnesses, but you do not give yourselves time, the medical swoops in and recommends killing you faster and more expensive ways, cancer is contracted and not, you have decided you want to pass from an illness but haven't decided which one, so you get a cancer, however that said let's just look a minute, there is a lot more to it than this so do not take this as form, Author.

Let's say you have a blood cancer this has been collected through many stresses though some children come into your world with this, these are contracted take my word for that, the soul wants to learn some hard lessons, and this is a hard lesson, one of least control if I'm not wrong, the soul has no control and has to rely on parents for care and treatment. So, if your parents do not want medical intervention and can cure this with natural medicine, the governments would find you of not caring enough to let them sort this out and you know they will only give human killing drugs, your child is made a ward of the state if I'm not wrong, they take parental rights from the parent, where is this right?

Oh, I have given much to consider here the pharma companies run your world author and you know this, any other race would be snapping our hands off for treatments and cures. No, your world doesn't want it, the small the people want this, for they are the ones losing loved ones to these illnesses, the men in power don't simply care, now tell me you are not involved in this, author your people need to take back their power this is just one way you're out of the loop. The placements of space stations on the moon and Saturn is another. The Mars experiment is another, yes, a placed station there too. We live subterranean and yet so do many of your worlds, only this is not common knowledge, there are as many people under your planet, and in your planet, as there are on the surface, there are no wars, except with our races, off world. We want you all to wake up, smell the roses of your planet. It will be total disclosure as you know within the time frame of a few short "Years" many of you know we exist many are talking to you, and yet the "Spiritual" overture is taking over, but there are false teachers on your world, they are "spiritual" to a degree they are able to raise the consciousness of their students, and they do not push to get them further.

**Author:** *Why are you not visiting my hometown, why is this localised in the USA?*

**Dr Z:** Oh there are many plans to land on your front lawn Author trust me on that and this is not localised to the USA though many are there it's the biggest country in the human world, or civilized country, we know the "Irish" are an accepting forward species I want to say as they were the first country to allow gay marriage we know if we localise our showing to the few we can be more accepted their first, we know that and we are working with many nationalities, we will be visiting many states and counties in a bid to help total disclosure of our world, though we are also careful, as Ireland is also one of the most catholic and Christian countries there is, this belief will push out everything many of the people ever believed in, and would without a doubt cause a shock to the human people living there, humanity might be damaged however it would force a wakeup call, that again said we do not want to force us upon you, if you are living in a state of bliss what can we do. We do know it wouldn't matter if we landed on the white house lawn and got out to speak to the president, they would say it was a Hollywood. We understand that and believe it or not we do see a time when we are accepted as the norm in your country. Though I can answer truthfully yes, we will make contact bodily contact with you throughout time. I will not give a timeline on this for now.

We too are travellers via other realms, I can tell you as the realm we go to visit comes into view our race our beings, whatever you feel the need to call us, we get excited at the prospect of visiting friends across the universes, come let me show you into this.

**Author:** *How do you control the ship I Know it connected to the consciousness but how?*

*Also as we walk up a floating ramp of sorts the outside is grey metallic colour and sort of looks like spectrolite from the outside, it has many colours, for the most part, its breathing and yet it's not, as we walk inside we are not on the floor it's almost like floating along, and one feels lightweight, and in front of me there are three aliens to the right side, and two looking at me but are a different race to the three, these are peacekeepers or a peaceful source, they don't know me so don't trust me.*

**Dr Z:** No author that's not correct we do know you

and do trust you, we see your soul light is not much different to ours. These are the normal they are always here when we bring others aboard. Yes, we see soul lights as a matter of knowing who beings are come and keep explaining what you see for others.

**Author:** *the first two are blonde hair to their shoulders wavy, with white robes but not robes, it's like a long suit jacket and then trousers, they look like guardians and look the exact same with blue eyes, Pleiadeans.*

*As I get all the way in the ramp moulds into a door it's like liquid metal, the two blonder guides, turn and walk down a long hall or corridor and it's like a haze has gone over the sides in front of me and to the side its very weird it is like walking in a bubble you can see everything, you know when you watch a film and something goes invisible and it's a wavy energy of clear fluid, this is what this feels like inside but we can see everything outside too, as we move down this corridor it feels like I'm walking feet above the earth and we are outside only I know we are not we are inside. Then towards the end of the corridor a reptilian sticks his head out of a door, he looks like a t-rex head, but he smiles and pulls his head back in the doorway, and I hear him in my mind, "Sorry", but he is smiling that there is weird. Walking further down I see a group a few a lot of people coming towards us, headed their feet are like goats' feet and hairy legs, oh boy.*

*They have robes on long robes, and they are chattering I Can hear it in my mind, someone said: "Over that terrible music" that makes me laugh.*

*Their heads are like goats too they are I'm going to call them goat men, defiantly feel the male energy to me, their robes are dark green and have a long top on over Alibaba trousers that are also like a khaki green. They have clipboards, and Dr Z said into my mind they are students like your earth world they hear to learn.*

*As we arrive into something that looks like a fully fitted operating room, and in the sides of the room are huge shorelines or look like that they have other animals or things in them, and the room is no longer see through though there is a bed of sorts for someone to lie on, That's enough for today I can't work like this anymore my head is sore the consciousness of something in that room has spiked a headache.*

**Dr Z:** we will come back to this tomorrow Author, your next guide for the next part of this channel is in there, and yes, your head will be sore tomorrow morning, but it won't last, and please make sure you eat before we work at 11 am. Then around 14:00 hours we will bring in the guide to help with the book, tonight your mind is too tired.

Good evening Author see you then.

## Races of Off-world Beings.

**Author:** *The greys are reportedly a soulless army engineered, they the scientists or whoever is on the back of this movement, claim that they are soulless because they are living one life, they have no place to return too. I know from recent channels this is wrong, Dean can you give me something on the "Agenda" or the theories behind this?*

**Dean:** Good afternoon Author later than planned but yes, I can and will answer, I know these questions I Seen them forming in your mind yesterday, and many more you have forgotten so let me get this out and any questions you have I will graciously answer.

The greys are a race of Alien, we are a spiritual race, we do not have an agenda, but same cannot be said for the smaller race of greys so I can explain this correctly. I need to show you who we are where we originally come from. We are a seventh-dimensional being and have been moving through the dimensions for aeons of time, many of us have long since passed, or left the body and returned home, our home that will be explained shortly. When the Greys where first inducted to the earth world it was a barren land, we helped many races with the development of the ecosystem, adding life to the planet the evolution the early man, the Triassic, Cretaceous periods the Jurassic, the lot we were there with others, mainly from Pleiadeans and Orion Sirius, Andromeda.

Lavias and other many other species of "Aliens" we all come together to work and grow the Earth world, and your planet is not so special, Author we have been doing this for a millennia and more, it is now that the people of the time know about us, we have been there or on your planet throughout that time, the DNA of the people the early human have many Alien DNA, there is no Pure race anywhere throughout the galaxy, no one pure race there is many DNAs that make up the race, the early human was hybrid with the species that looked more like the Pleiadeans, Lemerians and Andromedins for the very simple reason the human body would suffice for the planet you in habit all of us are suited to the planet we inhabit, Author, please I will explain this in simple terms to keep in line with the books you have written.

The early man was the very raw design of that blueprint, then we added DNA took some away, the only problems we ran into the was the brain, the human brain would have to be smaller based on the head circumferences, we decided as the mainframe wouldn't matter as the human was evolving the brain too would evolve, the only issue we foreseen was the "free will" no other living world has free will, this we didn't think too much about, to have an option there would need to be an option and there was no choice, early man wasn't all that smart so we foresee no problems. It's easy to sit here and tell you we messed up, but we didn't, the earth world has a blueprint of evolution, and it's been followed, to the letter. So, let's just say there is an undercurrent going on here with other races, there is a united collaboration of planets, the Intergalactic Council, of twelve planetary bases, we have always said we cannot interfere we can help, only if the planet is at serious risk, we cannot step in and help.

This has changed so very recently we can step in to help and are doing so daily, there is a secret government there is a society if you like running the earth world. It doesn't come from the greys, we are cloned. Yes, it's been that way for millennia but not all though most.

We are cloned for the reason our reproductivity is different from you, as the Grey procreates we lose the brain capacity, as its nearly impossible to keep the race pure, and with mixed DNA we proved that beyond a doubt to keep the high brain capabilities we have to clone, it's very easy, each body is inhabited by a soul, an individual. It's that way the only thing that is cloned in the biological body, the physical self, the brain is individual the body is the same as the next grey and so on and so forth. Many of us have the organs internally, and some do not need to be cloned. The most of us are. The soul of the grey when we die, we move on to our ***own*** spiritual world. The comings and goings of energy right now, is warning you not to forget the Angels, there is a reason for this, I'm working haphazard Author I know this, let me explain.

The dumbing down of human society has been an agenda by the shadow governments, it's been this way, money and power run your world, A race of mixed alien DNA with the reptilian races, and let's just be clear, not all reptilian races are involved here. I am not going to give the names as you requested but it's all in the eyes, the eyes are grey, or blue. Which about covers many of the humans in your world, they are power hungry and narcissistic reptilians. They have found a way to connect to the lightworkers, on the world and through this connection, they will attempt to have discord, Author this is a hard understand, and few lightworkers understand the off-world Guardians and guides. And even more, do not trust them. They are usually seen as a channel much like we do with you, a controlling ego. We see it as I am working with many high up in the angelic community to shut these connections down.

So now we come the consciousness of the human being is waking up, they are discovering us, and many like us, they are discovering many of us are being channelled. We are struggling to keep out the worst of us, it's hard to let you see the light of the situations while warning the many for you simply get confused on whom to trust, but it's rather simple.

Your guide will introduce us, a soul of trust will introduce you to your off-world guides and channels, we will give you honest information. There is a whole new world Author that the readers are not easily acceptance of because it's hard to see that your world is a dimensional world. And while you are simply sitting at your computer on the other dimension where the human eye cannot see could possibly be another being stood next to you, it freaks them out, and this is where the spiritual world of psychic protection comes in, if you are not 100% protected you are going to have invasions of privacy. Be that as a warning reader.

I don't bring in warnings for the sake of, and I normally do not do them at all. I see from my vantage point here many are channelling the "Aliens" right now, and there is a great push from our side to yours, the energy around your world is shifting, some for the better some for, the worse. The male/female divine energy is helping to keep the spiritual workers honest we are losing some to ego, they are the "Only" ones channelling aliens, and that is not correct, your angels are with you on each channel when you are working for the highest good, and the Pleiadeans are the easiest for the younger of fledging mediums to connect too. Lemurians are coming through too, this race once lived on the earth world quite freely. We took them back to the Lemuria when their world was lost, they left their DNA along with many other races to be brought back to the earth world. The reason much human carry alien DNA is the evolution of the brain for the upload of the consciousness, the human body cannot support the brain connectivity more than 10% and maybe a little more, over the evolution of time we are hoping the upgrades more of the brain will come online.

I say ten percent lightly, its more or less via the energy used not the proportionate size of the brain, each sector has more than needed vs neurons, I want to make it clear, ten per cent energy, one hundred percent brain matter. The human brain is made to be used the frontal lobe the rear cerebellar the parietal lobe, there are uses for all areas of the brain vs the bodies uses for them, the percentage we talk about is based on consciousness levels of the brain, the brain of the human isn't nearly as intelligent as it should be, however, it will be over incarnational timeline evolution and blueprints. I needed to clear this up. The human brain has the capability to be a superconsciousness living tissue. At present much is wasted as memories move from the memory of temporary to the core memory of the soul.

**Author:** *Was the earth world and experiment for the aliens?*

**Dean:** Not in so much an experiment no, we populate many planets, and none have free will, the explosion of DNA left behind from the others the aliens whoever you want to call, we had taken many off the blueprints we left behind the initial plans are still in order. The fact there is secret society's shadow governments with ties to the reptilian forces, and so on, it's not surprising, none of that is surprising, we have our old from Hitler to be grateful for this, and yet we knew it was coming, all he did was bring it sooner than we expected.

Many races are here on your world many malevolent races mixed with human DNA they look very human, living here on your world, many ships are travelling through the atmosphere daily and landing these are the best or worst kept secret humanity now has, the worst of us is there, and while they give out information about us, none of that is true to life hence why I am here and many more like me, from other worlds, the Aucturians are spiritual people fighting the races of reptilian across the dimensions next to us they have the biggest force of warrior souls.

Sirians, from Sirius, again not as bad as one would claim, they too have a warrior force, humanity will be caught up in this, while the majority of the human race cannot believe aliens exist the rest of us are fighting outside forces.

**Author:** *And yet you still have time to be spiritual?*

**Dean:** That is the blueprint the evolutional plan we stick to regimentally, the fact many of you are bringing through us in channels and readings right now, is no coincidence we are rallying to wake you up. It will not come as an alien force lands on your planet and show themselves, it will come into the minds of the many, and we start with the mediums the lightworkers and then the common man, this is the way we are working with this situation we have found presented to us. Let me start this again, in a way you can understand.

Many guides and guardians will present themselves to your lightworkers, they will be presented to you by your guides, and angelic beings, many of these are hybrid souls, many of these have lived upon worlds, we do not buy the "Fallen" this is a way of religionising something very simply put. Many angel's DNA is shared with us, with many of us, through the spiritual worlds remember; It was said our spiritual world is the exact same without the angelic beings unless requested, this is the way it's always, been, the soul of every being is an energy, energy doesn't carry DNA.

However, living energy does, this is where the biological body comes in, angels do not have the physical body as such in the spiritual world, they have physical looking bodies they have light bodies, they have energy bodies, light is reflected based on energy correlation connected to their surroundings. So in all angelic DNA shouldn't exist and yet it does. Coming to the Pleiadean planets is where the light DNA was extracted, based on energy, we have moved on a lot from the human beings so when we say energy doesn't have DNA we mean energy around the human body, the physical body, not the Angelic body, see I might have lost many with that simple statement and not you, it seems.

When the angelic forces join with the Others for the betterment of all its because they have incarnated, yes. They incarnated to other planets never have the angelic forces incarnated to the earth world, that worlds energy is simply too harsh. Yes, DNA has been taken from the earth world to others that are a common occurrence. So, in simple terms, the Fallen is again religionised by the churches to bring people under the thumb. The very Catholic church is behind a lot of atrocities, it simply wouldn't be me to leave it at that, and yet I have to, but I will say this, the reptilian forces are everywhere. And leave that at that. It is a lot for the human mind to sink, in. We understand this, and yet as the human mind opens and the questions come, we expect to be able to answer more, we are not allowed to give information without you are asking for it. It is a rule of our world.

**Author:** *How can one learn without you offering up information?*

**Dean:** You had no trouble so expect the other humans to also have no trouble finding information, where did yours come from Author.

**Author:** *You know where it came from you was with me.*

**Dean:** I was (He smiled) Then come on give it up.

**Author:** *Do I have too?*

**Dean: (Smirks)**

**Author:** *I watch a lot and read through dots, I watched something yesterday and the night before and read between the lines, it simple in this job to feel the truth of the world and remember the channels we have had without alien races, for these books, to read them lines too.*

*I remember one channel was told about energy manipulation for travel, can you expand on that for me please* Dean?

**Dean:** It's not hard to do Author, I will example the Aucturians as they are simpler to explain.

Their advanced weaponry and ships, their every day ships are made from well I tried to explain this before so because your mind hasn't got this I will explain in ways "You" can understand

There is a liquid metal that can be manipulated, as an energy source meaning into any shape without destroying the internal structure, of the shapes it started as, and the ship I am talking about is an elongated shape like a corn kernel on its side. The ship is large with a high based energy field around her, this is manoeuvrable by thought and feeling, it's very similar to the thought and feeling behind the spiritual worlds souls thinking robes, you see robes, see what I'm saying. So, with the travelling to other worlds, there is an energy around each planet, it would look to the naked human eye as the jet stream, and yet this is pure energy, higher consciousness energy. The ship's Commander would raise his vibrational consciousness energy to suit the planet in which they are visiting, and this is how they travel, but this energy is used by the Aucturians through crystals. These are off world crystals, not found anywhere one your world and specialist only to their world.

The things that are being taught on your world are simple things; nothing is breaking our rules right now because rules are only put in place at the top level. We are far more advanced than you are, we dip in and out of the future, but like I Said we could not change the future of the Earth world from here, it needs to be changed by each individual piece involved in it. It's these blueprints that we lend to the spiritual world that lays down what each lesson should be in the world when you incarnate; this will make so much more sense when you are home. It's almost like looking at each planet and knowing you can only help by being there and knowing that each section the blueprint can only be assigned by a single body, a lesson you must come not just for humanity but for yourselves too. This is what incarnating means, for you and for the whole.

Many of the Pleiadeans are hybrid with the Angelic realm, many more are hybrid with the spiritual forces of Greys, and many other worlds it's the only way we can maintain the specific needs for the worlds. Us we, the greys we have a smaller grey, and then there is the main which is us. We are as I have described energy manipulators, we can appear as whoever appeals to the being looking at us, or we are just who we are, we are simply able to do it better away from the earth world, and we do not go there for the joy of it. We go to look at and check up on life. We take samples and add samples, we remove the animals that are being killed off, and we leave the ones that are thriving. This is why the animal planets are thriving we move them out of harm's way and leave them better off, your world has killed off so many species just simply living.

The smaller grey is the grey many of you will have seen in your world; they are the ones who come we rarely accompany them, this is where we have been taken advantage of.

**Author:** *Why do the greys crash on our planet if they are so highly evolved? Why do they crash at all?*

**Dean:** There have been some highly developed scanners put up into the atmosphere, around the earth world the Hubble scope has a jammer on board, designed to jam many systems it comes into contact with. And as we have evolved so have you, many of us were blind to what was being designed on your world, and many of you are. You used our world against us.

For the most part, the crash landings have had systems jammed when they enter the dimension around your planet, we do not come the same way that the human comes back from space missions. We do not have to worry about entering the atmosphere and burn up to our ships, we come in via the portals of energy littered around the galaxies, through dimensional energy shifts. as we come through some are interrupting the signals, how else does one explain the authorities getting to the ships as they land?

But you do not have to take my word for this Author, we do have another Alien wanting to come to speak with you, I believe you know him from a channel from recent reading. He works with energy and also our Zealon wants to come back to work with you. Jonathan has already introduced you to us, and Author he his energy is staunch to the point, it would do well not to joke with him.

I know you can't help yourself with that. But please remember the Others are not used to you, or working with you, so cannot understand the "Joke" we will also be bringing MF to work from the spiritual world. To have someone from your own team working with this energy. I understand this is alright with you and this will be today Earth time, and I request six pm your time.

**MF:** I Understand more than you think, about why it's just so hard to believe in the channels you're doing you know author. It took me a while to get them too, not because I didn't believe but because I did, and how many more would think I lost my mind. That said I really didn't care when you realise the world isn't what you have been led to believe, first comes the mistrust in the system, then comes the (*Have I lost the f.... Plot*). When you realise you have not lost the plot, you then start to ask the questions, you're at the next stage. The first time I took you to channel Dean, and your head almost blew off I remember then, and I laugh.

Dean lost his stuff and called me pretentious, and I was, I admit that I was very pretentious. I am well aware of the timescale author and was trying to push it along, I'm very sorry.

**Author:** *It doesn't matter now, and it didn't matter then, it was fun. However, I have respect for them, coming to work with us, or the other ways around. I do however think that this Alien adventure is a little scary for me. I'm not scared, I am thinking how far down the rabbit hole I can go, or where will it lead me. I know I'm a writer as well as the other stuff, I want to get the books out and the other books, people have been remarkably understanding, that said I need to get this out. So many other channels channel this so why now and me why Am I doing it?*

**Medium F:** Because somewhere in the depth of the past when contracts were made up soul promises was agreed on; this was agreed on, many aliens and guides from our spiritual world decided at a point in that future some truths would need to be delivered and why not from a star-seed soul themselves. The star-seed souls belonging to the animals is a hard swallow, for many and yet this is your world, also. So, let's begin I want to introduce you to another Alien the one responsible for that incredible headache you have built at the top of your head, and yes, the animals will sit down as the energy shifts.

**Author:** *Is Jonathan around; I feel his energy.*

**Medium F.** Very perceptive Author, yes, he is around to the right of your shoulder and your guide to the left you feel him, Gabe do you not?

**Author:** *I do, I feel four guides and others.*

**Medium F:** Yes, four guides and others. Let's begin we are late enough this evening you are a fidget author,

**Author:** *Sorry, the dishes needed to be done and I was hungry, and the dogs and cats come on let's work.*

**Medium:** Here to the right is Zealon you know him, already and call him Z for the channels. Next to him is a reptilian guide from Zealon's planet and yet he is not. He is a peacekeeper you met him the other night or one of them anyway.

Beside him, is Dean, and to the right of him also your right that big cold shoulder you have is coming in from this guide, he is a guide, and he is from Andromeda, and one other from Arcturus.

**Author:** Why so many?

**Medium F:** Energy we are holding it for you so you can work with them, and yet splitting the work into two instead of one is just right. Rhaji will be along shortly.

**Author:** Can I please use the names of the planets for

the names of the guides I Simply cannot hope to remember names?

**Medium F:** That is alright Author, and yet we will work that out at a later date so yes, names of planets for guides till you get used to their names works because you will see who they look like **and get used to them.**

**Author:** *Thank you who first?*

**Anzia:** I am Anzia from Andromeda, and I know you said planets but let's try with this first, or call me A I do not mind, I come from this star system, but I wasn't incarnated there. My skin is off green as you see, but I can manipulate that to be any colour like your worlds chameleons. I blend to background again depending on what is perceived to become a threat to us, we are a spiritual being, we have no agenda on your world. We come only as Dean said to help, we were one of the planets that helped populate your world, the grey the smaller greys we have names for, we do not call them big Greys and small greys, like you would in your world. From here in Andromeda, we call them the Sapient. I believe in your world it means the Wise because they are. They are the work-force behind the larger of their kind, they are also the scientists the doctors the animal beings they work and can blend their energy with, that of their occupant and look into the body by becoming transparent. They are not the only being that can do that, their skin looks translucent, and you still see their shape, this is adapted over time, the time on a world like ours is nothing, the spiritual world has no time. We have no time, we do not have to be anywhere for a specific time, it's relevant it always has been. If we are talking a pregnancy, then that is a time rate or length, or however one seeks to measure it.

We simply do not bother. Now our world we are open to helping others across the galaxies, we also are a world where we have many plants, trees, flora and fauna. I called on earth, or palaeontology, your language is so much different to ours and yet the translate we have a device instilled into our brain, For some of us. Its only added when we take on missions of such it means you do not hear us how we normally communicate it gives us your voice, our voice box isn't developed we do not have this. It's a major difference, simply because mind to mind communication is the norm for us, for you to understand me we work this way, this is almost like a transformer of sorts. No, author, it doesn't hurt going in.

Animals on our world are souls the same as every other world, we have some very different animals compared to your world, and yet you wanted to know are all war animals star-seed animals?

Is that right?

**Author:** *Yes, it's correct.*

**Anzia:** Some are yes, actually the majority of canines you have worked with, and will continue to work with are star-seed, the reason here is very simple, your energy can read them better than that of the other animal kingdom souls. And yes there are many animal worlds, but there is only one true Animal Kingdom. Or world, it's a dimensional world where souls go back to from each world, each planet no matter where in the universe or dimensions they are from the ultimately go back to the Animal Kingdom. And their soul is just like you have always worked with, author they are kind just there is no badness, and yes J**** is star-seed, his high energy reading is conflicting with the body he is inhabiting right now, and no language barrier is blocking his education it is solely an energy conflict. I can and will help with this soul, Author because he is unhappy and yes we do not think to stay in the environment is going to work long-term.

**Author:** *So, why was he allowed to come?*

**Anzia:** You were totally correct at the time of seeing him, and yet off contract got him to P****d, this will always be to his detriment. His DNA will prove him incapable of not being in conflict in this lifetime, his contract is only that of pro-creation his life expectancy isn't long on this world, and yet while he is there, he has an important job of teaching the human to change the negatives of that mind. This is alright for a while it will make them physically ill, you are what you put out, and that soul is not a mean soul. They are a light being a soul from the planet of the Pleiades and along with her twin flame.

And yet this energy invite will hurt this union, this special couple has some hard lessons in this lifetime, we were only ever able to show you the earth world incarnations for this couple, but rest assured in this lifetime you will take them back off world. Only when they are ready to accept this, and it's not yet for one of them, and the other one is already there and accepting of it, however, tread carefully Author the energy will be helped with the crystals you have sent there. I will have helped with that and now is the time, I wasn't allowed to come help before now, there is a timeline for everything and all things. He is hiding energy this never ends well with animals feeding on this energy. You will have notified of this.

Every animal has a DNA that is compatible with the body they are using, I know over time you have found some remarkable instances, animals remember past lives on each planet as well as the earth world. And yet major injuries from lifetime to lifetime can call into question is it worth them remembering? Lets going to a horse you were working with, she was showing all signs of lameness and yet no physical injury, this was one hundred per cent correct when you said she is past life injury, the only difference is the past life injuries are harder as an animal to cure, you trick the physical into believing you are treating them with herbology an the body does the rest, you never forget the extra chakras and where we told you they were for star-seed animals, clear there and the animal is well on their way to be coming back to full earth world bodily fitness, it's a simple technique and the human is struggling, to believe in this work Author because they will have to admit there is more to the world than what they allow themselves to believe and yet they believe in the power of healing and only when they need it. I do sound cynical but as an animal guide from Andromeda we see assorts of beings struggling to believe in us but believing in the magic of energy work and her healing properties.

I attach myself only to the healers working with the psyche of the animals; all bodies need to become involved in the healing author as you know, healing only the physical will not work in the long run. Now we must move on.

**Author:** *What is your job in the universe aside of animal work, what do you do as a being?*

**Anzia:** Our world is as complex and as beautiful as the next worlds, to the outsiders looking in, we are an energy planet, we rate at the fourth dimension and closer to the Pleiadean than another world. We are a hybrid being, coming to your planet often, we are closer to watching you we had tried to be inconspicuous however when the Rosewell case happened we were already on the earth world, we rushed to help however we couldn't do much the human authorities got to the ships before we did. We also can absolutely tell you Dean is right the system was jammed, the technology the human now have based on what they have learnt from the Sapiens is too much for them to even consider how to use. They are trying and have long since been breeding their own aliens with the hope of one day creating a trojan horse, however the main stopping of this is they will never be allowed far enough into the realms because they would absolutely cause untold damage, they simply cannot keep their own beings under control we will not let them out of the galaxy. I will move along now, author and pass you over to the next guardian of their planet. Good day author, I will be back along to help with the cases.

**Author:** *Thank you Anzia.*

**Author:** *What's going on the planet guys, we know something is, however as much as I would like to remain on the spiritual aspect of this, I know I'm being taken down a rabbit hole, and yes, I Know a headache is coming in this channel so please someone enlighten me?*

**Medium F:** Author you know we can't give you everything, because that is all known we working on the mostly unknown so the under the planet fighting yes, we know about that we know about the strange noises across your planet, we know the mutilations are human not Alien its highly offensive to ask that question to our neighbours. Though I understand why you would. But before we go on, let me bring Dean in here to give a response to many of your questions.

**Dean:** Super gate, is a gate or a portal in and out of your world, and no it's not a "super gate" there are many portals in and out of the earth's atmosphere, many are opening daily earth time, the fact of the matter is these are not special, so blow that one off your list. Animal mutilations are not done by any being off-world; they are done by earthlings, making them look off world. This is an offensive question I know you didn't ask it for it to be that way, I know you know its earth people are doing it, it's a conformational question a yes or a no, it's a no.

Loud Noises are us coming and going around your planet, much of our travel is super quiet. Though if you like the supersonic boom, you would sometimes have heard in the early 80s when the the sound barrier would have been breached. When we come in via certain entrance points these noises are heard, it's the same going out, more so if more ships are exiting or entering the noise bounces off nearby ships, making a grinding noise sometimes, other times is very different noises heard by the human ear sonic sounds, and yes I can say they are all us. And others.

Your governments are setting the Earth world up, it won't be set up as we have done it to give us the disclosure we require it's going to be set up without them knowing we know. It's going to be the biggest failure in history, they want the earth's population to know about us. However they want it on their terms, they are going to make it look like we are enslaving people, it's not in most of our natures.

Again the Arcturians are nervous, that they human is setting themselves us, a cover-up Alien story, to have a human look to The Government to protect them, from themselves. This is a very real concern across not just one of our planets but others in the galactic councils, I wish to see it play out.

The underground battle with some reptoids is very real, this is the big bad wolf of off-world, and these are the excuse needed to show you earth people us in a bad light, we never mind too much about that, having access to the future scenes this will not end well for them.

Also, to show many of you dead and to bring you under back under the proverbial thumb, of being so grateful to them for saving you, you will be drones you will have no free will, we do not want this. It is why we are pushing into the minds of the spiritual workers,. It leaves that when the worst happens, you will know us.

The USA, UK. Russia, China, Mexico, Canada. Ireland, many of the UN countries are wholly invested in this, only the USA military are alone in the fight with the underground Entities we have just spoken about, we wouldn't trust them at all. There are no natural weather storms and superstorms, Harrp and Cern, and many more have a hand in these. The global warming doctorate is being brought about not by Many natural disasters, but by the people of the planet couple that with the government's plans, come on why would the head of the USA not believe in global warming unless A. He is incredibly stupid or B, he knows the plans behind these groups that work with the weather.

Though we can go with A also.

These are and have tried to clean up your worlds atmosphere, and failed this too along with many weather planes have been going up and looking at stats based on chemicals used to raise global temperature. I know Author unbelievable the fact you are still channelling us is a normal good indicator you believe it.

**Author:** *I don't need to believe it to write it down if you tell me it exists, I have no backup to claim it doesn't mean I will put it down.*

**Dean:** Human artificial intelligence is a no, we do not like it, these ai Robots are all fun on the surface however they make compelling drones. But thinking for themselves is really not possible unless they add in a super-consciousness, and this is where this is headed, they are working on transcendence, this is happening in factories across the USA. It's not good it's a super soldier we do not want it, and neither do you, where do these ideas come from? Have you asked yourselves?

We want you to remember the timeline, from spiritual awareness and this, this is a whole new ball game. Think about its readers. It is in the here, and now, we know they are heading for full disclosure of our world we want this, though it's not the full disclosure of the Alien life forces, they simply will not give it all, a base on the moon a base on Saturn and a base on Mars. Many will blow themselves out of the water. So now readers close encounters of the third kind are living breathing, and we are heading for a war with the humans based on the lies told. We doubt any of them know the truth?

Blue Avians yes there are humanoids, that have been watching your planet for millennia of time, watching your grandparents and parents and so forth for a long time. They are a kind Alien/Being if you like. They want you all to know they exist they can improve your planet with medical advancements and technologies to help fight cancers and illnesses, your world is not just ready for this information. Though they are, and yet the human being can/could live in total peace with these Aliens/Beings. If only your planet didn't love war so much, nothing is ever peaceful its always over land, we might not have lived on it, but many of us lived in it, the Earth world does not belong to the human soul, the earth world belongs to the stars.

**Author:** *What else can you tell me I don't know? I know I don't know much, but I have heard many conspiracy theories and believed My brain can't take any more, so what else can you do for my wee brain?*

**Dean:** I see your point you didn't want to learn this did you? Though you came to work with other planetary beings, for spiritual world work, readings and whatever the case may be, I know the inside of our ships and biologists you love so we can work there.

Author can we take you back to the ship you were on last night, but please we need a meditation from you before this to relax your mind to enable you to connect to this particular elder. Their energy is way higher than mine or another being you have worked with so far so we will direct you in while you stay wrapped up warm the cold draft is coming on through right now, and just keep concentrating while we chat alright,

**Corenthaiaslek:** Zanytabelterranian is the name of my planet, is shortened term, please stick with this author, I feel the head, I was based on the human make-up, I'm not human I am many beings by genetics, I am from a cold grey planet when the portal is opened this is what you see first, then as you move through the planet its red stone and sand much like your Sahara desert, there are many "Men" or beings look like men we are not, but we are close to your own being as possible, our brains are much more larger though our heads only slightly the spinal column Is solid and the consciousness connects not only to the brain but to the spinal column it's this way we connect to our living enterprises, and this is how we connect to many technologies they connect to our spinal cord and are grown this way, the microbes connect through the conscious mind, my level of energy is much higher than that of your planet Author, and thank you for allowing me access to your mind, to bring this channel this is done through telepathic communication.

You are remarkable easy to connect to, though I know it was uncomfortable for you, our world is much like the red planet as you can see by looking, Author, my partner in this life is over 7ft tall, and that is the way they are we are similar to the human in body condition that's where it ends. We also can talk through the vocal cords, but rarely do, the look or the mind talk is enough, here then we have given birth, as male but only a few of us can do that, and the rest are the human way, we lived on your planet many lifetimes ago, we made it home and returned back to the stars when the world went under water and froze, many of our people are still under the ice, and yet many are happy here, there is not a being here that doesn't have someone under the ice, your timeline is much different to ours.

We are a fighting force when we need to be, and yet prefer to live in peace most of the time, only when we are threatened will we take the fight to you. And lately we have been staying out of that fight, not because we won't win, but because many families are involved, and we want no part if this fight with the humans, much of your DNA belongs to us, we are fair skinned, like your white man and over the millennium we have remained that way despite many infiltrating the gene pool, our closet neighbours are reptilian and we have good race relations with them.

Our technological advancements here are limited by our own admission we didn't want that, but space travel has kept us up to date on these things only.

The rock around our world is volcanic rock, with a small subterranean connection near the south side of the planet, these are for the most part the fighting force that makes the weapons of choice here on our planet. I leave you now Author come back again, and we will explore the medical facilities here as they are extensive there is nothing we cannot fix, I have been training many from other planets here. From AI Limbs to birth of our young.

Here is where you need to be, and Dean knows this.

My name is Corenthaiaslek I am happy to help with this author please do come back.

**Author:** *I will thank you.*

**Dean:** Next one Author. One more just today then we work on your book.

**Zee:** We are a reptilian force and reside in the 5th dimension not overly far many 3.2million light years from Earth and half that again. From Corenthaiasleks planet, we do programmes from their world to ours for fighting and other exchanges of knowledge. They are our closest allies. We help them grow foodstuff they help us with medical advancements, then to help with breeding on our world, as many of our species are male, and few females, the females are let's just say, I do not want to offend you as a human or a female?

But they are not as easy to get along with, as the male of our planet we also have hermaphrodite/gynandromorph bodies on our world, and of course, these make up our rearing force. They rear the young ones not raised by their biological families. We live on the surface of our planet and farm subterranean, we are an industrial planet where the from the surface it looks peaceful no farming in much of anything, but we make the living metals your world would call them, they are like carbon fibre of your world with titanium like substance that grows, integrates with the body and stops the need to breed. When working in our military it stunts the growth, so we have to make sure we are fully equipped with the right working and living metals, this information we do not want the human to get, they will abuse this, the humans have no great how do you put it? No great reputation across the universe, we agreed with Dean to show you around our planet, for you not for them.

So come human, this is where we can work together. Down here it's warm and sees the ship we are in the middle of connecting up to the Captain. Here are two, there one for each section of this it's a medical facility much like your Red cross, we fly to many different systems as a force of good. Though we will fight if we have to, it's rare we will do it. Or main primary goal is healing through the conscious mind, and adding official Artifical intelligent limbs that connect to the mind of the individual, though making sure nerves and core cells are protected long enough that we can get to them is paramount, we have a substance the re-fires the genomes needed to re-light and stimulate the nuclei in the cells. Helping us the attach the sensors that will connect to the conscious mind. Then into the superconscious mind, it's a simple technique, and when discovered it brought the councils into one of the sectors to convey. Hence the Offical, though found between Corenthaiasleks and here we both get to keep this as long as we can use it for both planets and the intergalactic councils. We are allowed to use the main portal near the base to connect to earth should their come at a time, you need this information for good only.

**Author:** *Will this technology ever be allowed into your world, unless of course, you come up with this yourselves.*

**Zee:** This and the living working connections for joints we were talking about for the animal's Author, this will be allowed under the same regulations when it's perfected.

My planet is called Sarasasholazyte, in the human language that's as close as we will allow this information to be. We are in the main metauniverse like I said 3.2million light years from Earth and half that again, from Corenthaiasleks planet.

Just call me Zee. And I come for you human.

**Author:** *Thank you, Zee.*

## Intergalactic travel.

**Author:** *Dean, or other higher energy guides, where are you when channelling to me here? Are you in the spiritual world or are you on the home planet, your home planet?*

**Dean:** we are always on our home planet my planet is outside of your star system and outside of the twelve under the inter-galactic advisory council. Alright, there are twelve you know that who incarnate upon the earth world but there are more than the twelve who help populate other worlds, and we are all under and intergalactic advisory council. Author, I get this I am trying to put into easy to understand words for the readers and for you to understand as you are not educated in this. There are many within your governments and outside of that totally understand, but the majority of people in your homeworld just will not get it, you have nothing in your language that helps with that, so I am trying, and I see we are struggling right now so please bear with me. I am from a planet which would be as I said outside of your galaxy; and from a higher vibrational plane, which means we have to come back into the 4d world to come to visit, and we know your own planet is ignoring our being around.

Seeing as we cannot communicate fully with the main people or the heads of governments, we come in via telepathic communications, for aeons of time, there have been many instruments available to your homeworld. However this information we give is not allowed, or should I say censored to the majority, and while any information I give will not impact it might help. There is nothing we can give; we will not give the technical information needed to help your planet figure out how propulsion to and from diminutions, we will not give planetary details on how to navigate the galaxy's space travel is so simple and yet your own inventors. And others are making it difficult, As the present and future are so closely connected to us, we are incarnating our own light beings to your world.

You are so far back even via blueprint on your planet; inventions are back, the medical inventions are backwards. The scientific basis of inventions is backward, anything you see during the walk around the spiritual world the interviews with Einstein and the interviews with Who was Tesla? Your behind based on the fact we show you everything, and yet you have no basis to compare it too, so we send our own light bodies to your world. To bring it forward at the present time your over thousands of years behind out technologies, and yet when you visit our planets we are behind you; in irrigation techniques and biological diversities and imprints. Energy bodies are working we have minuscule tips we can give to your mediums and channeller's, the animal world light beings and veterinary scientists are stepping forward to help as we know the medical advancements of your world are being held under lock and key and until a brave scientist steps out from under the thumb of the oppressors. There is nothing to be done. Many have returned to the homeworlds after giving information out, and we are not about that, we get that the medical issues your doctors have spoken about are very true we even helped there too and with the Amazonian peoples.

Take your HIV crisis. The world people are pouring money into these medical awareness's and programmes, and yet nothing is coming out of the labs to help, or nothing was. We see where the breakthroughs have been made and these are locked up and investigated, I'm sorry medium there is not a lot we can do to help your world you are all under the thumb, and there nothing the governments won't hide from the majority. Reasons are all down to what they call security and money; they want to hold power and the keys to the Earth. And yet the people are working like ants and objects to cover the governments, there is another planet aside of your own, that is similar however there is no free will, and you might say you have free will to make your own decisions and then look at the choices and see how suppressed you are as a people. What's allowed and what's not and then tell me you still have free will; the people are treated like worker ants.

**Author:** *You don't like earth people, do you?*

**Higher guide:** No. I do not, the majority no. They were born into a free race and yet they are allowing others to take over, have you any idea how many "light beings" incarnate to your world because it's a free world, and yet your suppressed? You as a race are petty, and your bullies. You are destroying your own world, and you expect other worlds to be able to give you the intel on how to get off your planet and into wormholes to take you to our galaxy's and help you. Did you know how much space-junk is in your stratosphere? Do you know how? You know don't answer medium I know you do not know.

**Author:** *Mmmm not sure how to answer you. Do you guide other humans or just sneak in and channel who lets you?*

**Higher guide**: Medium/Human. I talk to and am allowed to, be channelled by star seeds only.

**Author:** *Then the Human remark was you getting your galaxies in a twist then wasn't it.*

**Higher guide.** *(Nothing no answer)*

**Author:** *Have you quite finished and we can work?*

*He is walking around in my mind's eye and called over by Dean my higher guide. I see them talking in my mind's eye. The New guide shakes his head, and Dean is telling him off I'm sure of it.*

**Dean:** I'm not medium, he is a new trainee flanking other to get the feel on how to work with other planets light beings. I brought him with me, to have a channel with you, we are working with other planets guides the new guides, you are better for channelling atm as not many are channelling higher guides right now, I apologise Medium.

**Author:** *Dean I figured something was amiss He is a funny guide, let him stay I don't mind. His energy is giving me a headache on the left side by my ear. Ask him to tone it down, please.*

**Dean:** The wormhole work we have been doing across the galaxy not far from the red planet, we are joining with the animal guides right now and bringing animals across-to help repopulate another relatively young planet. I'm showing him the fauna and rock formations across the Red planet to help with that along with the people, of the Red planet they are simple people you know this, and we are going to be working in the labs shortly come,

**Author:** *I don't know what's going on my head is blowing up I'm sure one of the guides is interplanetary, somewhere I haven't worked because it's the energy that causes my headache and yet I'm used to working with Dean now. And of course, goose pimples are popping up, and I am yawning that's a shifting of energy around me and normal for me with certain off-worldly energies. Hahahahhahah sorry for laughing as Dean asked me to hurry in my mind's Eye we are standing outside a lab, and I have seen these before just never been inside as the door opens a man steps on in his light being energy and yet he looks like Einstein. Tickled me pink he did, I didn't expect to see someone like that, and yet as he stands in front of me, he welcomes me.*

**E.** Welcome medium. I was born, and we have worked before and what would I be doing in the labs on the red planet? I have been here a while I enjoy all aspects of life, and the biological environment here is unlike anything I have seen, and as NM follows you, I will be following you here also, come let's look at the samples we took today. In the red slides are simple internal rock samples that are collected from the nebula system. Though the gases are making it harder to collect them; and while the scientist here have an idea what they are we are taking samples, to study with the scientists of tomorrow. You know Medium, not just mediums are trained In the spiritual world you know, Many ***tists*** are trained in, I call them that Medium they are our physicists our, scientists, We is adept at Quantum travel here now too. And though we can go with just a thought; we are not travelling like that so come. In the green slides for use under the huge molecular system under the microscope, we have many plant slides, but we found a vein substance like tree sap but thinner and less milky in one of the prehistoric ferns, that grows on the other world with the animals on, you know the one you where there. Along with many other slides, we are bringing students here soon to look at the planet, and how it differs so, it's similar to a field test.

**Author:** *I know who you are, and I laughed because I didn't expect to see you. I am sorry.*

**E.** I laughed too. Your face. This is how you would have seen me in my earth time, and during our interview, and yet look now this is me as a soul in the spiritual world and how I show myself to the students; because many are incarnating within a short space of time. And as you know we present as a human to those souls as it prepares them for their incarnations or should I say as humanly like as we can. My light body I still look like I did in my last incarnation and it wasn't as you see me. In my last incarnation I was on one of the twelve planets a small planet over from Orion; not far from your own planet and yet similar, as we land come I will show you from my mind to yours. We will not go today author I know you're tired, and I know you prefer Author to medium, so I stick with that, come, and this is my last incarnation.

***Author: E.*** *will you describe it or will I for the people reading this.*

**E.** Very well, my planet is dusty and yet yellow and bright there is a lot of sand upon the surface, and the surface is hot, and yet as you know many other worlds, we live subterranean and yet this world we do not, she is much like the animal world, but we grow foodstuffs sub. Our power comes from the universal wind that's is quite strong around the northern side of the planet and yet il give you in your language understandable terms. We grow veg and harder substances that are beaten into a juice or a watered down, like Slop on your world and yet its easily taken on ours it has all the body needs there is no eating for the sake of.

The nourishment is taken in, and we add various fillers for our younger generation of workers as there is an order on the planet there are communities and families or groups, and there is an overseer. We are space travellers, and we build the transport many of your people see in your world, we use trans-dimensional travel, meaning we are able to appear anywhere based on the intelligence of the technologies we use. We do not take advantage of wormholes and black holes, we use energy manipulation techniques to move across the galaxies, and it's simple in all its simplicity. If you know the workings of the energy your using and yet the energy around the earth world is similar not as similar but not dis either for the trans-manipulation to work. The propulsion techniques that your world is trying will not work over long distances, and the gravitational pull of your world is heavy, you need to move to an oceanic area of the earth base and use that along with the lack of gravitational energy from a magnetic effect by the lack of, through the oceanic floor base. Simple and yet I know I haven't given enough information though you see it don't you Author?

**Author:** *I do yes. It's just past my pay grade, even typing it up I get confuzzled.*

**E:** We can only work with you as your consciousness is moving up and the more it moves, the better information we can channel over to you. See the way the craft lifts straight up; we have it on the level system it's a simple thing no matter which way the craft tilts, or flips the floor structure will always be level for standing on. And this is the main in the craft it was an internal structure build and crafted for the various degrees we are shifting at; there is a pull only as we lift from your earth world Author as no other planets have the same pull. It's almost like **"The grumpy pull"** some of us joke. But only the souls who have incarnated world earth can get that joke. Its black matter within the atmosphere around the earth world, its designed to vibrate at a different level to the earth world and yet keeps Earth In the dark, the majority of your galaxy is dark to other worlds, you are across the universe from many other planets and we cannot leave you to your own devices. Do you have any idea how many crafts visit your world daily while you're all blissfully ignorant Author?

**Author:** *No,*

**E:** A lot. Way more than should be. We come into communication with some earth people who gather at points around the globe, mainly the USA and invite us with them to connect on a subconsciousness level. Headed and led by a Doctor of medicine now in sciences, and a co-conspiracist, according to your so-called truth givers. And yet the doctor is a medical doctor, he is fighting a losing battle getting the governments to accept his work, many will break from the hiding of the truth and give testaments to his work, and yet the overall coverage is not given as the USA governments are doing what they do best. Cover it up, and yet his work will seep into the consciousness of many who go to him or hear of him. The shadow governments are there. Author marks my words. They are a shadow of what you have and a law unto themselves the moto is no one knows so we are answerable to no one. How can there be a law against something that isn't there? I leave for this time and come back. You are tired again I know channelling from higher consciousness causes sore heads author. We will learn to shift that energy for you.

***E.***

**Dean:** Very true Author and our own travel is similar and yet a little more than E's crafts as we are further again, though the technologies we have for consciousness time travel is helpful while talking to you. It gets my messages straight there and yours too it's like a bounce system this is why your head is sore, normally we would both have the same technological devices on, and while I was incarnating, we could do this and now I'm dimensional free-flying, its mind to mind or my mind and help to your mind. And we are working across the galaxies teaching students your world hence the soul that came this evening I apologise Author for his stupidity.

**Author:** *Dean no, he wasn't unlike you at. First, I get that, so we leave it at that he can come back.*

**Rhaji:** I Will work with you soon.

**E;** We do not need to incarnate to experience these things, we can travel to the Earth world very easily by skipping through dimensions, and through space walls like black holes, and yet the earth world does not understand the black hole enough to use them for space travel. The dimensional shifts it would take to move from one side of a galaxy to another would have far too much G-Force on the human body thus blowing the body inside out, it's not pretty, but the human must learn these for themselves. We cannot interfere. If the scientists of the time, your time, author I hardly believe it will be anytime soon, and yet by copyright of said books they will need to seek permission of this information and us giving this to you now ultimately gives our Author permission or not it's for her and no one else to decide. G-Force on the body the human body going through black holes is so powerful Like I said it's the inside out its very like the microwaves of your planets cooking utensils.

Author your work is pushing the boundaries from one

life to another the science in each will become more apparent, and yet we still have many asking to come work, now I introduce, ***Dennis.*** He was an Astronaut upon your world when they did the flyby the moon of course.

**Dennis;** I

was on the mission that performed the fly by; we were meant to be doing a lunar landing and the stabilisers where down, when Nasa came over the radio to perform a fly-by, Armstrong and myself picked up a signal as we caught sight of the lunar surface, it was almost like Morse code but not. And going back in the days the radio signals were sharp but nowhere near as sharp as your 21st-century radio. The lunar west side was showing what looked like water towers and obelisks that we had of course seen before form the tracking pictures on satellite, to see them up close would of cause leave us gasping, we were effectively looking at the irrefutable evidence there was life outside of our own solar system. Nasa was running scared; we were not allowed to talk about it; even voicing it to those in command who was seeing these things as we were tried to say what we were seeing was, of course, put there by the Russians.

Laughable huh we knew not, we where aware of the "so-called Dark side of the moon" and yet on the landing when Neil stepped down onto the lunar surface we could see, and though it was live it wasn't it was being cut, let me just say it wasn't as live as the world thought it was. A cover-up from start to finish, there was visible evidence we were not alone up there, and so it was also very obvious their capabilities far outweighed ours.

**Author:** *Did you really go to the moon? Can you tell me that off world beings inhabit the moon, and surrounding planets and was Nasa warned to pull out of the space race by the Russians or did the other world beings warn them to stay away?*

***Dennis;*** Hang on a minute you are aware that this information is classified?

**Author:** *You are aware you're Dead, and it doesn't matter?*

***Dennis;*** For a human your very smart, of course I know I'm dead, I'm talking to you am I not? Classified is just that, Dead or not it's the same though not in my case you see Author, I talked about this before I passed, they called me a whistleblower, and by now your aware Dennis is a fake name are you not? *She nods her head,* of course, she knows our Author is rather intelligent. Alright no more messing about yes, we signed NDAs when we signed on for training and only the best of the best got in and it's the same now; we cannot put people into space, and no know there is life on other planets. I now know that said life doesn't want to be how will I say it, it doesn't want NASA and the rest of the Earths superpowers to get off the earth, but that's too late, they don't want you out of their own star system, or galaxy. The earth people have made such an awful mess or their ozone layer of their own planet there is absolutely no way we are allowed to conquer space travel. I know that we have been warned if we do that the other off-world species will take us down. So where is the momentum in trying, and we cannot simply announce to the world we have been warned to take care of our own planet before seeking others, the worst kept secret will be blown wide open? Many millions of human souls are star seed souls, all incarnating to help bring the earth world up to scratch as a suitable planet and yet the failure rate is so high, right now. Humans of the governments around the world as hiding much and most of the research; of their own planet and yet we cannot expect the Aliens to let us have contact with theirs. Again I will reiterate something one of the off-world guides said this time last week to your Author, the governments are lying so much about us, that we will and are connecting to the Humans of the planet one at a time. We have been watching who is suitable to carry the message without actually announcing our arrival to the millions and billions and causing mass panic; we are not in your face you are channelling us. We are meeting with fractions of earth people of the planet and on. This was said only a week ago, many humans are channelling off world guides, and yet we are careful who, for many humans also allow their own consciousness to cross-contaminate information by allowing their minds to get in the way of the channelled information, you give it and leave it at that.

# 6

# OFF-WORLD TRAVEL WITH EIGHTEEN MEDIUMS AND A REGRESSIONIST

I MET, AND WORK BEGAN WITH A MEDIUM, WHO WE NICKNAMED MEDIUM F. OR MF.

**Author:** "From I said I wasn't giving any names my guides and yours decided we needed one."

**MF:** "So, I have chosen just one, and I'm Medium F I know whatever I give you will be fine, so we will move on,"

"I know you know me but for the work, its MF Agreed?"

**Author:** "*Agreed. Come on.*"

**MF:** "Can you see in front of you the golden waterfall? we go there first."

**Author:** *"This is from MFs point of view and channelled any other will be labelled as such, and all my notes come in as Author. Just as a point of reference for readers."*

**MF**: "We come into visit the golden waterfall, and many call the other things I call it that as that is what it looks like It is, of course, the healing waters of the higher realm. Your Author has some issues with her health, and we will step into this water in hopes the soul will be helped, and much healing goes on from here for her human body the joints give her many issues, but she helps us anyways as it's her purpose in the life."

"We step into the water, and it's neither cold or warm. It just is, and the bottom is pink rose quartz suitable to go with the healing. We also walk through this, and many souls are around watching our progression, we might end up with a few stragglers as I do not come here this often in the "day" with another soul who is not a Medium or learning this. On the spiritual side and of course your Regressionist is causing a stir, definitely not his intention that said they would know him from his work. And many of the souls not here that long, with a glance over and come and say welcome to him and the Author."

"We hang around only as long as we need, we are not on a time limit, but I know your/our Author gets tired and might need to break as she is earthly even if she is here with us."

"We step into the grassy area and many other Mediums, we know step forward to shake hands say hi and clap each other on the back. This is "Medium central" I never envisaged coming as many souls would be around, it seems they know we are here. Not much different happens around here. So, when visitors come, many come to see many of your older mediums who have passed to spirit are here, working away with students of the day. Many of the earth famous mediums are here, and we know our Author will not give out names we know that, so no one is shy, and they all come."

"Read this, and you will know who comes as the names will pop up in your head, and then you are correct it's lovely to see how they come. And many students turn up too."

"We move around now we must press on we head to the higher stations where, the higher guides and guardians will be we know Gabe and Johan and Havern are already there they await your Author for we have many accompanying us on this journey today, so expect many names popping in to this section of your book. Many you will know from earlier."

"Guides such as Havern will help with contract questions and so on and so forth."

"As we come to a taller as it is wide building its white like a library outside with four pillars and ornate wooden doors that are propped open for our visit and inside the station is like the library in the Czech Republic and the cross between it and Hogwarts to my mind's eye. I know others describe it bases on what's in their mind's eyes. There are many students in learning here, and many have just stopped as we came in. Authors guide River the Indian guide, comes forward takes her hands and rubs them "it's nice to see you again my friend he says" We will be leaving shortly we gather the number of souls needed for this expedition, and we are a total of eighteen for this group, and we are headed out to the Red planet first the nebula has been broke they can get through with Wii fi connections, and we are visiting there too"

"On this planet, the rock is reddish and many other red issues around it, but it's not the real name it's the name we give it for our scientists, and it seems to stick with most of us we know it as the red planet. Of course, it's not the same as your "Red Planet".

"Many of us are now ready to leave."

"We are now standing on a backdrop to the ocean, and this is a water planet many streams run into the main ocean, and the water is used as electricity here. The bigger plant is inland, and the plant is mainly underground, and only the vague amount of buildings stands above ground as we also use the water here to irrigate the underground growth stations for the food grown on the planet, the fish are not taken out as food this is a vegetarian planet no animals are used for food. We also use solar here for other parts of the planet, but we are not visiting them today we come to see the mammals here and the crustaceans in the isolation section of the planet. We are working with them in the growth stages, and they are used for repopulations of the planets and Johan will be stepping in with Gabe here. I work with the animals here and on other planets but know nothing about the ecosystem."

## Johan and Gabe.

**Johan.** "Remember we spoke about the ecosystem on the other red planet and other planets and about restocking them using biodiversity and thermos technologies and other."

"We are doing the same here though, this planet is more or less as populated as we would like. Some of the crustacea in other areas have exploded, and for the most part, we have let them, as we have so many more planets to fix. These little guys eat worms, and the like and leaf base compost for breeding in, that said of late the temperatures coming in from the solar areas have risen around the plant, and we didn't expect that thus said it's been a breeding explosion as the earth is warmer the crustaceans who lay in the soil and plant base planet floor. They are or was in the early stages of progressiveness, as we had never seen some of these on this planet naturally, these are water animals, for the most part, not anymore.

They have come onto the land to breed, we knew they were different as we were studying them, but when they didn't breed in captivity we left them alone, we do not have a specific site for them in captivity. We were studying them in their natural state, when we moved them into a laboratory set specific for them, we knew they had lungs as such what we didn't know was these develop only once in the lifetime and bring them to the land, as land animals and they breed here. Then in the rains, the larvae of them get to the streams. It's all very complicated hence the explosion of them as we brought them in as young all together instead of in stages like growing lettuce. Also, that said they all matured together the ocean creatures and mammals see them as a delicacy, and we still have a mass of them we do not know what to do with. We have decided at best leave them to their own devices as natural selection will take them out or let them be."

"We know some mammals like them. They have no defence mechanism. They do not have claws as such; they eat on land and in the water, the land-based diet is full of fat, we do know they eat only worms on the surface we do know they eat ocean greenery in the water. We know they will eat rotten fish in the water too. Our studies of these creatures have been a long study, and we have decided to move some to the red planet as an experiment to see if they can withstand other environments."

"We have had a massive explosion of these creatures, crustaceans whatever you wish to call them, and we have many souls looking out for them here. The developmental stage they might have outgrown themselves and might not make a natural selection. This would be a shame as they really are a cute little creature. The basis for them was we had the perfect ecosystem, well its proven to be too perfect, so now leaving the ones we do not take to the Red Planet here. And let nature decide the rest we will work with, in other areas away from the solar areas on the red planet, we have set up the scientists there already to work with them."

"Now we go on, these little creatures we also have some strange mammals living in the waterways. None of our animals attacks the inhabitants of this world the souls here are looking rather odd to "humans" they are equipped with the body suitable for the planetary systems they live in. As this world is part of the spiritual world and not the Ets although they look alien to you and me and your guides and mediums from the homeworld of Earth, they are who they need to be for them."

**MF:** "These "people" are extremely friendly, and many can astral travel back to the spiritual world as they grow into their soul's. They all talk telepathically with each other; there is only the young that voice vocal noises and these are laughter crying and screaming, the normal emotional responses of the soul."

"While this worlds inhabitant looks odd Author, they hear your every thought. They do not get many earthly visitors, in fact, they have had only one before, and I have worked with him also."

**Johan:** "I will explain to your readers again what is going on, Eighteen souls came with us including us or altogether I mean, we were on the backdrop of the ocean and we have now moved inland to the underground paths of the "Circle of light" where all inhabitants work underground but many on the surface, it was created as such as it is cooler underground. The heat is not unbearable and is a steady heat. It's of such the programmes when we first got her set up growing foodstuff and factories of such underground; it just stuck we found most foodstuffs underground and digging out the cave systems was easy enough with the machinery we call the mole for this operation. It was easy to maintain and keep operational when we were over-heated on the surface."

"Your readers will be amazed at the planets in this multiverse of dimensional worlds as they will see them as a fictional science world and there is nothing, we can do about that, souls remember the spiritual world and only now are some remembering other worlds. The block from other worlds is much stronger than the block from home. The spiritual world is home for all."

"Even the souls on the outer worlds belong at home, and these worlds are populated, there are Seven multi-dimensional worlds. We populate many and many more we do not, but we help with. And a few within the region of the spiritual world where we live as souls as part of the spiritual world. It is not complicated it's just you are, still under the illusion of there is only Earth and the spiritual world, however, as our Author, you are allowed to know that this is more accurate than any other soul you know right now. I'm sure many more will come around in time, or many other guides will decide to tell their students that we are more than. But for the meantime, we are happy as we are.

Many spiritual teachers need to know this information, and it will be out as we need them to teach connections to the likes of this world, they work as I said as telepathically like the spiritual world and there will times when they join your guides as healers. This is a programme that is getting underway so let's say in five-ten Earth years many of the people from here will be joining with your reiki healers and angelic healers as the circle of light is a powerful healing tool from this world, and many can weld this as it's in their DNA. Much like your Mediums and Authors and inventors. Much work needs to be done between the guides and our healers here. To channel that through to the Humans upon the Earth, and we will be teaming you up shortly to see if you can channel the mind of one of the inhabitants of this world. And no not today but on Tuesday we will bring someone from here to the spiritual world and will work with MF. And you so make a date Author. Until then we will not be showing them to you as we want you to "see" for yourself."

"Many healers here from the "Circle of light" will be animal healers and just a smaller fraction for the people as the healing is strong, and at this point, we cannot justify using it right now. There is a balance to all things, and we even us from the spiritual world as guides and guardians must know to keep the balance. We do use some of their gifts around the other planets as healers. This is the best Healing planetary people, (they do not mind me calling them people) They are also advanced in there thinking too much more forward than Humans are."

We move on.

## The Red Planet.

**MF: "**We are heading to the Red Planet",

"We come through the nebula, and in all its beauty it is beautiful, and the planets that come around the rock formations and rock deposits coming in to the planet that way is hard for some and not for others, not this time for us, and we will be meeting with some of the "people" here and they are people they are human in appearance and again talk and they too can hear minds and talk telepathically however many do voice their opinions, there is a huge castle type we are looking at there is also royals as we know them the society is much like the Human Earth but they are more advanced in their thinking, and all are the same no poor and no rich for its not money they use. It's based on love and loving each other, so all have enough."

"There are growing foodstuff here and the same no animal-based diets, but the animals do eat other animals but only for food. As you move further into the planet or further into the depth of the surface of the planet, some of the animals here are like our earth animals, and some are not, many are colourful, and some are plain, the elephants here are like ours at home but they are telepathic it's the advances of the Animal kingdom they are higher souls, again we can talk to them they can understand us, the only ones not capable of understanding thoughts and feelings are the collective souls of herd animals and some prey animals, and they are not all here most are on other planets left alone with no other civilizations around them."

"Connecting to Elephants souls are no different than connecting to the soul of a guide or guardian."

"Moving with the times we will head into the castle where many inhabitants live, there are different clans or societies across the planets, and the head of most of the scientific communities live here."

"We do have some stranger than fiction inhabitants here, and these people are for another time, we will not let them be ridiculed by adding them here, and the Author knows that these people have already been included in the set of books before and the Author has not realised she has channelled."

"I know this is now sticking a lightbulb moment in our Authors head and so it should it was partly that book that helped the idea of this one become cemented when we requested her help. Some Authors can sit channel whole new characters and "stories" and not realise this is what is happening, and this is the beauty of a character open to our world."

"We will have to come back tomorrow our Author is struggling with the arm issue, we will make sure healing occurs, we cannot take it away as its soul contract, but we can help that it doesn't interfere with her writing. We will bring NM the regressionist of course with us, he is having far too much fun to leave him behind, I know with his mouth hanging open on each section of the planet we go to he is even amusing me."

**NM:** "I never knew this was here in any of the case studies this never came in I'm totally blown away. I need another life writing about this stuff. I can't believe why didn't I know?"

"I understand Johan said no one knows no one remembers, but holy hell. Oops sorry."

**Johan:** "Nope NM you will never write about this for this is not the soul path this will get out, and people will know, you will and can request to come to these worlds to incarnate yourself or just come to work, and we know you want to it's all over your astounded face."

**NM:** "I can't believe it, I have been in the spiritual world for a while now, and I never knew. How come do others know, ok don't answer that? I get what needs to be done, and come back with the Author is that ok? Johan?"

**Johan:** "Yes. We have requested your assistance in other chats too. If you will allow us to indulge in your interview techniques."

**NM:** "Yes, Oh I'm so excited why are you not excited Author?"

**Author:** *"NM I will be tomorrow I'm just sore in hand, but my soul is as amazed as you are, I feel I have been here before, so it's no great shock to me."*

**MF:** "Come let's go home now."

We come into the higher realms again as we head back to the teaching station to drop off some of the guides and stragglers who came too. All blown minds today and we will catch up tomorrow.

**Author: NM**. *Tickled the life out of me during that channel he was so excited, but it opened up a question. As soon as I had another reading with Jonathan, A guide channelled with the UK medium Elaine Thorpe I asked him, "Jonathan I said why is it that NM Had been in the spiritual world for over a year, and hadn't known about off-world planets?"*

*"He was very gracious and said that Just because He lives here, he is still learning too, and he would ask again could he accompany us off-world when Working, and of course he did. This astounded me. To be given this information from Jonathan and again through the regressionist.*

## 7

## ARCTURUS

We are heading back to the Red Planet today scientists there are waiting for us.

We call her the Red Planet as her base is red Dirt; the mountainous areas are mainly red with black and green moss that grows there. The surface of the mountainous area is damp from the water that runs under her, but the surface is incredibly warm, sulphide runs through the rocks, and while the steam that is let off smells a little off, we have found there are no unstable areas. We are as scientists looking into this as it should be at least slightly combustible, but it doesn't appear to be.

We have taken the samples to the labs and found that even the lightest spark goes out nothing seems to cause issues with this, and now we are looking at why? Sulphide is a combustible substance in the right quantities, are we too much over or not enough? We know that the oxygen on the planet varies, from which side we are on; that's why we inhabit only the west side the other is too close to the heart of our people. We tend to struggle so this is the main reasoning we are going with for now, but we will be investigating this closely. We know much about the surface of our planet here, it was one of the most tested and yet intriguing planets inhabited and connected to the spirit world. And yet we still allow others from closer planets to come to inhabit with us and join races.

Those that can breathe only the air qualities are left to the west side, where the oxygen and nitrate are at the best content for us. The others who are able to breathe through the sulphide and oxygen are left the south side, this too affects the animals who walk and live on the Red planet we have overgrowth on the west side and smaller in the Southside. The Others as you know have their base, and this is the base we will be visiting this time. You know I have worked on this base before its massive and the right amount of Oxygen and Nitrate is pumped in circulated with their own mixes that work for them and they live within the confines. Author we know you do not have a brain capable of understanding many of the mixes of chemicals that help the others with their breathing so, please do not worry about us putting that upon you, we give you only what you can understand. Come let's walk.

You see the trees over here are almost blue like the grasses; this comes from the air over here. The bark is the same as our own, but the leaves and grass so very different. While ours change colour depending on wind direction, our people breathe just fine. The slight variations in the air are soaked into the grasses and plant services to adjust the colour slightly, if this were your earth world, you would never notice, as your eyesight is not strong enough to see those changes.

Come. You see the compound from here along with

airstrips as you would call them. They fly in only; the spirit people can come in as we do.

YOUR FRIEND DEAN HAD WORKED HERE BEFORE WHEN HE was an incarnated being. Along with other scientists we are now more an understood planet though still young our eco-system is stable.

Many aeons of time working with many others, Johan and Jacob also helped with that; and where are more able to help you understand. The Nebula was the main call for the others to come to see as you know. By looking and as you have been told it doesn't work as it should, even with the gravitational forces at work. It is still moving the opposite of what is natural and what we would deem "normal." Earth scientists are amongst our most confused when they reincarnate here. Of course, we do not call them that often but when their core learning has them so totally confused we do, and they laugh with us. You have to take what you learnt in other planets and throw them out of the proverbial window, this planet is all, what would you call it, erm Yes Topsy Turvy all your normal is not normal here.

**E:** THIS IS MY PLANET, JUST ONE MORE CHANNEL AUTHOR then I let you finish up. This was channelled a long time ago, by my friend Arcturus he is from Aucturia, we never did get a name from him when we channelled the above statement, however He still is incarnated with me up there, I have been back to spirit and back again into the labs where you found me that day. We will be working with you very soon Author, I must remind you to bring forth the channels from the Animal planet for the next book Author. I go now and have a message for your readers.

I thank you for giving these books a chance, when I incarnated in your world, as a Mathematician I loved working with the planets, and I now know why, star seed souls are us, who look up to the planets and know we do not belong on earth. ***27.10.18***

# 8

## ONE LAST CHANNEL WITH A FRIEND AND SOME OFF-WORLD GUIDES

A**uthor:** *Drawing to the end of this Book a book I never expected to write.* We decided to keep the most of the off-world channels separate to the spiritual world channels, and yet they all connect so it was hard to bring only one or two over, however as we were wrapping this first book up. The regressionist, I loathe calling him that, he is more like a friend after all this time, (*He is here smiling of course*)We had one more channel and invited with him a couple off world guides to discuss, well you will see.

### *Chatting with MN.*

**Author:** *You live there now and have been there for a while, what has surprised you the most?*

*Also, in your opinion why are the LGBTQ issues a bugbear with many higher guides? Or Aliens. Also, can you give me anything that will help our world and the work of the spiritual people? Or the work I am doing, I know many regressionists don't value channeller's so why did you come to me?*

**MN:** Good afternoon my dear welcome back, we have

had some fun since you have been gone and yet not gone, you have taken me on some very fun planets, and off-world, off-world in spirit form is just amazing its planet hopping. Spiritual selves are a much higher connection to the light of the universe but let me answer some questions for you, and then we can do some of mine if you do not mind.

**Author:** *No, I do not mind, I have spoken with some on the group and answers always answers, and yet I saw you broke bread with well you know who I'm talking about. I don't want to mention names.*

**MN:** Yes, I do, and we had a good chat though I'm very sure you haven't seen it and only heard about it am I correct?

**Author:** *You are I don't want to influence any work I do with you over the work you did there.*

**MN:** Rightly so, R is a nice genuine guy one I'm proud to know and call a friend. Now let's get into your questions,

**Quote, Author:** *You live there now and have been there for a while, what has surprised you the most?*

Not in so much surprised me as when I first arrived and went through the process I was enlightened enough to realise I didn't get much wrong in my work, though the credit doesn't come to me it goes to my clients, without them the work wouldn't have been done. We wouldn't, couldn't, have even begun to understand the magnitude of the world in which we live now. Not your world of course ours. The spiritual world is on a higher vibrational plane of existence than that I first realised.

The ascension into the higher realms is taking time to get to via the routes we know of. These are incarnational routes of course, and yet I have seen time and time again that these are not specific to anyone. And you can, of course, ascend by staying here or moving into higher dimensions and incarnating onto many of their worlds. And yet I see your working with many on the planets now.

I'm not going to name them Author I know it's not needed, and as you are not working here with me this day, I know too that you're missing the work with us as your prepared to ascend once again. The hearing and mind activity at night-time the smells and tastes, the energy feeling off and the less and less company you seek is a good indication of that, now in answer to your question and aside of the obvious. Our planet hopping was something that totally blew me away. I didn't know I could and never thought to ask until you showed up here with your guides in tow, and took myself and seventeen other souls off world, I know you questioned Jonathan about that, and yes, we are doing it a lot. I will always remember that it sticks in my soul memory we are working with as you know the Healing planet and the energy around said planet, enabling the "Humans" to blend energy it takes time and will take time.

Though as you know, and it was explained between five to ten earthly years before we have this on the earth world. And really when you see this as a quantum healing therapy, you can and will understand why we see what we see. The Regression therapy you participated with the bone problem on your own elbow, you will be able to show the way. Understanding and knowing where the problem came from a can and will heal others. Though we are not in any hurry to bring this forward from the healing planet because your world hasn't fully embraced going back to come forward. Pin down the where the injury came from and you will have your ability to heal, just like when you pinned down the animal's whereabouts and good work Author, that's a breakthrough your world needed.

The second question, The LGBTQ Issues are not so

much a bugbear as you call it, more of a symbolic issue. If you cannot love your own differences why not how, can you love theirs? Many races in the trans-dimensional worlds are one gender races and not because they are sexist but solely it's the way it's always been, you know the genetics or the biology I heard you went over this yesterday, so my reply is, how can you love yourselves and not love others? Please, your world is more than these issues, but this was the main brought up because many world races are one sex one gender born as and it's never thought of again because it doesn't cause problems as it does on the earth world.

Ok, now male races we are going to greys, we are going to the fraction of Sirians, who live within the main race of the Sirians and yet they are the working group if you like, like drones and workers from the bees and other insect colonies, they are stronger able to carry out work and so on and forth. This race is especially watching your earth world, knowing that many won't understand their biology they be highly offended Author, that your human world will not "Like" or agree on them because of a something that never is called into question in their lives. They procreate as Asexual beings and also bring in donor genes for diversity. It's clinical yes, it gets the job done if you like, but its real and they have feelings so no they will not entertain Earth people. And yet not all earth people, Spiritual people from Earth carry a vast diversity of beliefs, and therefore they are highly sought after to channel their world and your Doctor M, and Z you work with are from this very planet these very beings.

The reason I came was that you subconsciously asked, you needed the voice and opinions of two regressionists, and while there are many here you know our work, you know us. Throughout these books, you have had many guides, Doctors and so on and each with their own opinions of our world, this way working with who you know of levels the playing field if you like. You work like I do not reading material to sway your work, you worked by not understanding what you were and still are getting and jumping in both feet together to give it your best shot. And while I never understood work with twin flames, I acknowledged when I saw you did I not?

**Author:** *You did M, and it wasn't expected it was never expected.*

**MN:** No, you absolutely correct it wasn't expected, but I felt I needed to validate as much as I don't like the almost bible like expectations of my work. I understand it gives a bar in which to move on from, while my work was and is breakthrough much of yours is also, you took what you knew of my work and expanded on it from the Animals soul point of view. And this hasn't been done before, and this is where we are today. Animals souls Author these are the ones that are crying out for help from your world to ours. And yet while the soul of the human might feel they are sentient beings, they are highly unfair to many animals. Many of the animals in China should be sent home their plights are duly noted, their lives are not in vain now ask me some more questions I like.

Our Q and As and we haven't had one for a while, though ask me something you think I can handle, just because I'm a dead regressionist it doesn't mean I have become Einstein.

**Author**: *In your opinion why go back to a past life, what do we have to gain to look into these? And are they very beneficial to our lives?*

**MN:** As a regressionist I would, of course, say going back into the past helps bring one's life forward, you have read my book and yet seen many cases of people "stuck" in their lives and trying to understand the meaning of contracts and learning to move forward without bringing baggage or karma with them. Or find out if you're alone, I know we are not alone, and yet when someone becomes a client for a session; we would chat for a couple hours first and foremost. I get to gauge where their lives are now, what they are looking for, questions to ask themselves from former lives etc. Now Author if you could go back and tell yourself something let's say just sixteen years ago what you would say to yourself?

Huh because these are very similar to going back into a past life understanding who you come with and why.

Finding out information can help you understand the life your living now and come on Author you have done past life readings and never get the same life twice unless there is something you haven't learnt. For example, your own past life, you found yourself in a Roman Generals body twice in the same scene the same lifetime and yet both times where different, tell me, Author,, this is where we helped with your arm isn't it, because you where that shell-shocked the first time when the connection was made to your twin flame, that at the point of death when you both passed together in each other's arms, you never noticed the position of the arrows did you?

**Author:** *No, I didn't.*

**MN,** and yet that was the most profound and healing that was misunderstood, so when you do these past life readings, you get that many of the healing and moving forward can be found at the point of death from one lifetime into the next, or into the life between lives. This is another when you take your client into the spiritual world and interact between lives, you are able to see their guides, and the contracts are drawn before and now are you not?

**Author:** *Yes, you know I do.*

**MN,** Well then as you know as well as I do, many Anxieties and traumas from one life to the next bury themselves so deep into soul memories, that they can be carried over. Even if you do not remember the exact deed; that caused these traumatic memories the Soul memory does. It's fragmented causing reactions to triggers you might never even know you are triggering, this brings all manner of reactions. Anxiety and phobias and bad dreams all manner of triggers that are felt by the soul memory again but not remembering why this is where the past life readings and life between life readings are useful.

**Author:** *Can you explain why only some lives are shown, not all and why not? And why if I did twenty past lives on one client that each time unless as mentioned above am, I only shown certain snippets? (For the readers please)*

**MN**. Yes, Author, of course, this is my speciality, and yours, of course, l will explain.

As a human being despite not being as attuned to the universe as many beings or us, for example, light beings, and spirit people. Etc you are connected so deeply into the energy of the universe and yet still not, as you do not have the memories of the soul, whereas you go for reading for example. Or you get a reading done like you do author and the only difference is I hypnotise you, you connect on the soul level so it's a soul regression of past lives and this is very profound if you are gifted with that ability as you are, so we move on.

As we tune to the life of the client, we ask the higher self, or I do, or you do. We ask them to show me/us the life that is causing the anxiety in this lifetime, and I'm shown just what we need, I take the client into the state needed and we go through it with them, their higher self will speak to me or the mind state it depends through the conscious physical mind. It isn't equipped to deal with this, the higher mind is more equipped. So we use this method amongst others, this lifetime, for example, let's just use an example say you were a highwayman (*You wasn't*), And your throat was cut with a blade, and in this lifetime you cannot pick up a knife, this is a simple explanation, and yet we can get deeper into this but we won't for now, you are taken back to the moment in your past that is causing the issues in this lifetime and I will take you through it, then if this is the moment of passing from the spiritual world until the Spirit world, we talk about soul families and so on and forth.

Now presuming this is the only issue we will talk you through it and explain that that was a past life it has no bearing on the life you live now, and the healing will occur. Its amazing Author when it explained and you re-live through it the release you feel. Now we know that we are only allowed to show you in this early regression, that which the soul is allowed to be shown via a spiritual guide that accompanies you. And again a trained hypnotherapist doing it this route is at its most important, the damage one can do to the human psyche if this is not performed right is immense hence we train only people who have training in hypnotherapy then we move to LBL training.

Now I will go your route, some mediums not all are trained in or have an ability to do, and yet I'm sticking with trained in. Because this soul regression is trained in the spiritual world when you're doing mediumship, Or Energy manipulation, its called Many things least of all Mediumship, however, it's a universal word you all know when you get home.

Before your birth into a body, this is a specialist training that the soul goes through and yet you didn't know that either did you author? I'm sure you knew why you can do it but wasn't sure where you trained so let me shed some light on your own training. Author I know you wanted to work with me from the spiritual world, however, I have been lucky enough to know you and well as you know me on a soul level, not meaning we are connected on a soul level only as ascension wise and consciousness levels, similar but not the same so we come back, I like this topic thank you for asking,

Now when you're trained here Author, and others like you. Your training goes in many different directions, if you're to take a lifetime in mediumship, we request you have as many tools in your belt as possible. Each lifetime leading to a Mediumship lifetime or lifetimes, you train in many directions as possible, many lessons many fractions to use in each life. For example ten lifetimes before your medium lifetime, your very psychic and then the next you are a card reader and enlighten in spirituality or drawing. Animal communication and scientific lifetime and so on and so forth all preparing you to be the medium. Or the Author or the scientist these lives are in preparation for this life. Coupled that with your training here for aeons of time, and you have the Medium, and you do not have to be a Spiritual medium author.

Being kind and loving and accepting of all, no ego and human. Is enough for a lifetime of mediumship and maybe in the next lifetime, you learn to connect to us, and so on and so forth till you are where you are now. Your own twin flame has told you, you're the medium I'm the writer did he not?

**Author:** *Yes, he did. Thank you for reminding me.*

**MN:** Alright I will explain to the readers how you read past lives. Two very different readings with two very different connections, you Author connect to the soul on a universal energy connection. Connecting directly through the soul of the client you get no "outside interference" you do not connect to the higher self unless you request this and though you do sometimes mainly its connection from soul self and your ability to go back, when their guide steps forward that accompanies them on this journey, you are able to request which lifetime again like me is relevant to the life in which the client is living. Though I have seen you work like this but connecting on multiple lifetimes, going back to the soul birth or just going back to the beginning of documented time, earth time and yet earth didn't always have a "time frame" this is simply reading from soul to soul, the discarnate self to the incarnate self. Heart space to heart space through the guide who will either stand with your own soul as you connect to the soul of the client and work this way or in the mind's eye as you see from that point.

As each reading is as relevant as each other, the only difference being my credentials are on paper, and yours are in the soul memory. This connection is a pure connection and yet trained for over a millennium of living in the spiritual world. Let's give a guided reading via the guide, now, for example, your guide and theirs's will step into the space allocated for the reading along with both spirit bodies you will connect to their higher self or soul self and the guide will show you their lifetime, and you will feel their feelings at this time.

So, for example here is one I'm sure you have connected with, the soul of the client was murdered in Atlantis, and it was me or the connection. If I remember right you were worried about giving the information to the client that they had indeed killed another human at that time, their spirit guide said no Author the soul is ready to hear this information not knowing to you that the client was going through some deeper issues of feeling a weakness of soul self, this solid evidence was to show the soul of the client is a strong person, they accepted the reading and came out stronger for it, this information was solid and therefore helpful for the client the overall reading was seven lifetimes all with a small bearing on the life lived now and ultimately the anxiety was found from which life and a small way to helping and other issues was addressed and yet you also explained while you cannot give a yes decision for your client you can advise where they have gone wrong over the past and why they are drawing the same energy the same lessons in each lifetime helping to make the lesson easier over time, this person I know went on to clear the issue and thankful for the past life reading she had.

And again, your animal regressions are breaking ground, the connection to foreign lives is groundbreaking as we have said before Author, and as we move forward from human past life regressions, we can help with the animal ones also.

**Author:** *Mn can you explain the use of colours in the spirit world, for soul levels if this is working or am, I missing something and or what you have learnt since you got there?*

**MN:** Author when you are standing in front of your own soul family, you can see your own souls colour the lighter, the higher consciousness or, the higher dimensional vibrational soul you are. So, it was always thought and yet its correct in some cases because there are many souls here from other dimensions it's almost like a standing station or a train station or an airport to where you need to be, but not always take the entry points, you've seen them many come straight in, alright let me explain this better I have been watching since my passing, and the start of my new life as this is a life. I have realised that I'm one of the souls that will be consistently reminded of this life no matter how many I go on to live. Immortalised forever due to the writing of my books. Not that I'm not delighted we opened eyes, I was just a man.

In the lower vibrational states of being or energy or levels younger souls, we know where you going when you come home, the guide or family members bring you straight to entry points, these are where family is waiting for you, without the massive landing stages, these younger souls are brought home and family are there, they recognise each other whether the soul colour shines out or not they know you, and if you were to stand in a circle you could see your own family colours. Multifaceted or light or not, they can see you, and yet not anyone's soul can. The light being you are or being of light, is a beacon to your own family in whom you're on the same level. Take for example many as twenty new souls are created or born, and you all come out of the nursery white, the energy you are animating is seen by all, whether they see it with the soul or feel it.

You are known as a new soul. Each level each soul has a vibrational colour, seen or felt or known we use the word seen, but mainly incarnated souls would use this word, and as we see you, we feel you. And so, on and so forth. So, I'm pale silver in soul colour and yet your pale blue very pale blue, and this again is a star seed energy that is inducted into the spiritual world and not you have free reign across the universes we all do, and yet we do not. We rarely move around a singular and rarely incarnate singular, you know your path for not just this lifetime but for others and yet you're so happy with that, and now I leave you Rhaji is coming in, I will see you again real soon Author.

**Rhaji:** Are you ready yet Author (He winks)

**Author:** *I am. I'm tired R and need some soul rest, please tonight take me home and rest my soul. Let me see some of our past.*

**Rhaji:** Author my pleasure. And now your animal

work. The animal connection you have is the same connections to them as to the soul that will be human, the Aucturians and Mintaka's and many from deeper Dimensional worlds are itching to get working, and yet I feel I need to forewarn you they are deeply spiritual souls that do not understand the jest of the human world. I know you, and Dean now gets on but remember what he was like Author I'm not sure even you can get them to talk like he now does. However, they are highly evolved that the delegate from Orion are your own people, or beings we are all from there as you know we are them, and them us. The Aucturians again do not understand jest either and are not giving credit to the laughter of your world. Sirians from Sirius and Astrelegains from the seventh-dimensional worlds are also meeting with us and guides, they are the science buffs Author. And have been working with your mind recently scanning to find out how to show you their advancements and yes Author the headaches where them.

**Author:** *Why did they not forewarn me?*

**Rhaji:** Why you agreed to work with them, and they are just doing what the agreement was, it's up to you to learn from them, the headaches you felt you will now recognise when they come through again, this timeframe on your world will be Thursday through Monday of solid working, please make sure you keep up.

**Author;** *I'm ready to work now.*

**Rhaji:** Your animals outside watch the weather, and we can work in the meantime. Let me introduce **Innkara** an Aucturian. **Inn-Kara** spelt like this Author. Please get it right. He is not like any other guide you have channelled. I will stand by now and help where needs are.

**Inn-Kara:** Welcome to our world, I have been pushing to work with you for a little while, please we come to help your world we know your world is harsh and the regime in which many of you are suppressed by but brought on by your own makings. The light of the world is growing dark in the hearts of man. We offer to help and been turned down by every conceivable corner. Your world doesn't want help at the top and yet the people the human in midlevel consciousness are crying out for help from anywhere.

We are aware your governments are only half a brain, or should I change that half consciously awake, they do not understand the world they live. They use their stupidity to make it sound amazing to the people who have no knowledge of politics. They are not playing at politics they are playing with control, and yet many are using the control to fuel hate across the planet and are getting away with murder, and yet murder of the spirit is murder also, a dumbed down collective is collective voting for them keeping them in office.

And yet even those rising up are only heard for so long nothing is being done, it all goes quiet again. This collective needs to wake up, we cannot penetrate the minds of the dumb, they have no thought process outside of their own, they do not hear us only the awaken and awakened. The higher consciousness hears others thought processes. The ones we instil into the mind while connecting to the Earth world, as a whole is picked up by certain channels. We offer a signal to all, and the few are attuned to this vibration, and this is who we connect Author.

Your guides connected to us and asked us to connect with you all, many more aside of you Author are working with us, and yet we are not the council of twelve we are the Aucturians and demand nothing of your planet. Offering help is one sided you have nothing we need or would want. Your world is dying and dying because you take and use and give nothing back, the small token of planting and clearing oceans and gleaning technological knowledge is too late a drastic planet of change is needed, for years your world has been on a precipice, and no one listens.

We have much to offer your world, and in bringing the science and the medical advancements we know we cannot offer them on a high-level clearance because the outside worlds and planets are not acceptable to your own, so we come in via the mediums and middleman if you like, we give to channels who write, and one can only hope the right people will collect the information we offer and guide with. We have many workers on our world who do not have free will, and yet they are from your world your souls the earth world incarnates and return then want to come to us, and we allow this because we go to your world, many karmas are brought back as many do not understand cause and effect. Though standing before a council then understanding we lose many more to try to come back and fix the karma. This we are working with to elevate so not more time on a dying planet, so now we have many who want to incarnate to help save and with the world that is dying many are readying for the next call.

The next call is the call that the planet needs help. Again. The first wave of volunteers. This is the second wave of volunteers.

This Second call is due to go out within the next Five earthy years. And yet I feel that is closer we are suspecting 2020 for that call, which in my council's agreements would be correct. Though the five years, instead of two was an estimate based on how the planet is coping. Again as we have seen the corruption of worlds and countries, we now are confident the 2020 call will go out. By the recent call that came was over sixty years ago. Earth years. And it didn't doesn't mean the first call failed, it means that we see more need again. The third wave of older souls are almost twelve to sixteen earthly years old, these will bring your world back on track, and yet we need back up they need back up. The second call wave of volunteers are the most important they came in ready and equipped DNA wise to get straight to work, they are no-nonsense souls. The carry the light of the world with them. They are to be known as the light bringers. The will be classed as outspoken, standing for rights and you will see the youngest of all inventors the youngest scientists the medical facilities they will bring with them and veterinary medicine knowledge these are mediums and teachers, scientists and doctors. These are Politian's to liberate the free worlds.

This Second call will lighten your world it's your worlds last chance. That is all I have to give you this time Author. I know this is special information please only Lee-Anne.

**Author:** *Thank you Inn-Kara.*

**Inn-Kara** Thank you, Author.

**Rhaji:** Mintaka's from Orion. Your home planet Author these guides know your soul self, our soul.

**Ashish:** Welcome Author, how are you getting on I see that I shouldn't have really asked that question because we see how you are getting on, this body this world you are trying your best, and as an older soul I know you yearn for home, Rhaji knows you yearn for home, and yet you stay to help. In helping others, they should be helpful for you should there not? And yet you're struggling with the need of earthly materialism not because you are, oh no because the need is there to do your thing in your life and without life is hard, and yet you struggle, we need to be sending more help and yet consider it done Author.

That is strange old friend, seeing you here and struggling, and again we admire the strength of character. I offered to come, I know you and your soul knows me, and the mind is struggling to remember, and yet I know you do. We know the soul is old and we know many struggles you do not yourself know favours my friend, you see around you no one does something for nothing, and yet you're always giving away your time. No, I'm here to put a stop to this. We send clients you do not give this away get your items sorted and your life on track then you will feel better in yourself. We withhold books going out while you realise waiting is not an option you need to be pro-active and take for yourself this is your next lesson and do it with no judgements, we will not judge you for taking what you need.

Now again, Author, the animals are working out for you here add this. How is that author?

**Author:** *I smile. If you think it will help, then thank you.*

**Ashish:** Oh, it will trust me.

**AUTHOR:** *ARE YOU AVAILABLE TO CHAT WITH MN, Rhaji, Dean?*

**Dean:** We are all Here you know how editing works by now Author.

**Author:** *Are you already to see the end of the books for a while?*

**Dean:** Laughing, where do you hear that from, no Author there is two of these, and one more of the Alive and Free, and the animal book, we will be channelling for the second one of these first then August for the alive and free, animals Feb. you remember now?

**Author:** *Bog off Dean, you're taking the M ain't you?*

**Dean: Nope.** (*Laughing his rear off)*

**Author:** *Oh, well just more in my head stuff, I felt sure youse was giving me a break till August! And just Rhaji would be around helping.*

**Dean:** Nope, get used to seeing my face, I will be

bringing in more, dimensional beings for this next one. Now I know you have a question fire away.

**Author:** *Don't say you weren't warned here.*

*I get the Equality for all, I really do, now going from this book and the others this was heavy in all three of them, explain this to me like I'm stupid. Also, surely the starving and third world countries only got one mention in these books, surely this is an important topic, along with many more. Considering it was you who mentioned this Dean at the very beginning of our work together. We have worked with doctors' scientists etc. throughout all three books, so what's next or why have they only thought to bring these topics in for us...*

**Dean:** Yes, I will answer the first Author, the Equality for all isn't just based on Lgbtq+ rights, we know this; so, do you, and I see your playing devil's advocate here. In your world and ours, mine and others off planet we are a male race. With not just one singular sex, gender whatever you wish to call us, it's not just based on who one sleeps with. Or doesn't, or who one is attracted to or isn't, it's based-on souls, the soul of each of us is a chosen by choice soul. The contract is chosen before you incarnate, what we are saying is this: Life is Life Author, body parts aside, this is biology this doesn't matter on the grand scheme of things, its respect Author, I respect you, and you me and we haven't even met in this lifetime. It's not based on the fact my race is male. Your twin flame souls are male, or the fact you are female in the body. It's equality in all, in the body in the soul and in mind, on the planet. We have said over and over again. If you can all just see souls, the world would be a better place.

Regarding contracts, these are the hardest contracts by far and only the bravest souls' step forward to stand in any lifetime knowing they are holding the space, the hate crimes the parental crimes, the inequality for all. It's time to put a stop to this across the universe, we cannot trust the

Human self with other beings of a single-sex environment if they cannot live on their own world without hate for the difference. Who said that LGBTQ plus are different, there are that many of us that the balance will soon be tipped, especially if you add up the races across the universe Author.

Now your next question man has killed more than their own species, by hunger than any other species Alive. This is not just a hunger issue it's a greed issue when you walk into your large stores and see food boxed up, do you ever think about the souls walking miles for water etc. I don't suppose many of you do, and again this is a souls choice to where you chose, and these souls are far more spiritually evolved than most of the western peoples. I cannot say more than that one this subject, do not fear author just because we haven't brought it to you, we haven't got it in our sights. We have other channels to come. Many spiritual channels will be bringing other topics Author more suited to their capabilities, we use the mind or the souls more suited to what they have done or lived within other lifetimes. I go now I know MN is trying to step forward. Good evening Author, And I will be back.

Dean.

**MN:** I see what you're doing also, and I can't really add a lot more than what Dean has given to you, equality is more than the same rights for one as another, it's about living in peace, knowing you can hold a loved one's hand in the street like any other couple. It's about not getting the worse jobs or being discriminated against by bullying politicians and others, it's about had the same rights in all things as "Heterosexual" people. We tend to notice that the prejudices are by a certain fraction of people, and we have answered that question in Alive and free one. And Two.

As souls there are no prejudices, I will play devil's advocate here. Remember the channel with the Romans Author?

**Author:** *Yes, I do.*

**MN:** I can see you do, let me remind people, you reap what you sow, or this was the channel.

**PR:** Author you see them coming in all laughing they have not been called to channel before this is to trust your case, the pain within your chest will clear its energy, please wait a couple of minutes while we try to settle the energy and work with you.

Going back in time to that far ago, you will have been there at that time and will have seen many goings on even from your time in the tunnels Author. We never hid who we were, and we were punished for it. Or should I have said we never were given the appropriate burials owed to us? Oh, we were interred alright, and covered with our fine things but we were hidden. We wore the dress robes of the day with the over the shoulder habitats, I think you call them now, they were off-white almost a dusty white. Yet with sandals they were suitable for the time, BC Ancient Greece and Egypt where going through some hard times, and Gueaus Heiat ancient Egyptian soldier was a greedy son of a bitch he made sure we had to fight for all we had, my people where suffering we were kept away from the fight for a long time, and yet we trained our soldiers well in the fight.

Swords we had to fashion ourselves and Battle shields we had the best metal workers of the time we had bronze axes which were harder to swing. Many came to our side oh we trusted but a few. We went to war with the best of them and came out on top, many of our best we lost, the ancients saw war many times; we fought over stupid things looking back. We fought over land and buildings and the best of the men, we fought for our privileges, and we fought for the sake of fighting. We dug out the tunnels and fought in them too, we were almost drunk on fighting.

The Pharaohs came in and helped to sort these battles out. Shaving the body was to keep fleas away no hair meant no fleas, but we suffered from the heat. The strangest of items we held back, the fashions and the greed, turned many into the savages of the day. Jeus was one of a humble man, he was top of his barracks and looked out for the younger fighters in, the earlier days where soft the softest where teams with the hardest young ones and trained together giving them someone to love gave them someone to fight for.

We have been told of the vanity to wear wigs, we wore them, and we wore many "fashionable" items we were vain, we had no idea. No one to look up to. If you were born to the higher families, you were looked after many of us were lower-born, and many of us died before we held a sword to defend our territories.

**PH:** We used the bronze to fashion the many items this was the start of the bronze age, we had chariots, and our men were looked after, women were the child bearers. Many of us knew nothing of the women we never saw them from the moment we entered the army. We slept on the floor on rolls, sometimes hide many times cloth, we washed in the river, and many waters were brought to the higher commissioners to wash. The horses for the chariots were often looked after better than us, now do not get me wrong here we were apt at looking after ourselves, and we were "well looked after" compared to many but we were in disposable force of muscle. We fought for our people, and we died for our people. We loved our people. Now, this is where we will look at your world now, you have peace across the globe compared to us. Many of your fighters are fighting the same wars we did, Political and for land, we fought the Serbs and lost and won. We loved within our own ranks. And we died the same way. Do not feel sorry for us it was life as we knew it. We were just who we were I know history favours your world we were not well known we were just soldiers. Many of them were privileged and stayed that way. I do know many of them are incarnated into your world many war soldiers, know to walk the streets of the USA Europe and other countries living lives and moving on in lessons.

Can I tell you the shock of returning to the spirit world after coming back from our lives in Greece and Egypt, for we fought on both sides, we died on one and reborn into the other that was our karma. We come today to offer council you do unto others as you do unto yourself if not this life then the next.

**MN:** Now remembering this channel, they both died in battle and came back on the other side of the fight.

In the earth world karma is the same, you will come back as the least liked because of your prejudices, its Karma, you will get home one day, and when your life review is over you will realize that this wasn't meant to be, you will judge yourself most harshly for the hurt you will have caused. When you find yourself plotting your next lifetime? Well, let's just say no more with no ego, even the worst of the peoples have proved not too bad in the life. (Winks)

**MN:** Again, I can't add more as Dean said this third world is not yours to channel. It's again a soul choice and not for these books even in answer Author. You were always set to bring through doctors' scientists etc. we have vets and more Doctors waiting to come work with you for the next time. We do know you have a timeline on your own books. This is where Rhaji comes in. I will leave now but not for long Good evening Author.

**Rhaji:** Again, these topics were given to you for your timeline Author, and you know why the readers now know why, and yet that it's personnel based on the findings out from past lives. Now we do have a timeline, and yet we are pushing it fine Author, so I will stand back and allow the time to come where you can get finishing. Dean is quite right. We will be around a long time with your work.

*They came from the stars'* we did, and so do many of you, remember this when you look into the stars from your earth world, for home is in the stars.

I bid you good day.

The end.

# AUTHOR NOTES

Thank you to Rainbow Danger Designs for a beautiful cover.

To Spiritual Medium and Psychic artist Lee-Anne Higgs for the beautiful channelled picture of star-seed children.

I became an Author by mistake, I didn't know until I was asked to work for spirit this would happen. And now it has I'm happy to continue to work for them, and with them.

Even if A particular guide, is always breathing down my neck, telling me off.

To our readers, thank you for giving these books a chance. After all, they came from the stars for you.

30107305R00125

Printed in Great
Britain
by Amazon